THE HEALING POWER OF GARLIC

Paul Bergner

Orient Paperbacks
DELHI | MUMBAI | HYDERABAD

Dedicated to my herbal mothers, without whom I would know nothing of the heart of herbalism, especially Jane Rodriguez, Cascade Anderson Geller, Susun Weed, and Sharol Tilgner

ISBN: 978-81-222-0219-9

The Healing Power of Garlic

Subject: Health & Fitness / Naturopathy

1st Published 1998
8th Printing 2012

Published in arrangement with
Prima Publishing, USA

Published by
Orient Paperbacks
(A division of Vision Books Pvt. Ltd.)
5A/8 Ansari Road, New Delhi-110 002
www.orientpaperbacks.com

Cover design by Vision Studio

Printed at
Ravindra Printing Press, Delhi-110 006, India

Garlic as Medicine — History, Heritage, and a Living Tradition

Ancient Assyria	Recommended for infections, fevers, diarrhea, to treat painful swellings, sprains — and as a general tonic. *Nineveh Tablets* *Circa* 3000 BC
Ancient Egypt	Used for treating heart problems, tumours, headaches, worm bites... *Ebers Codex*, 1550 BC
Ancient Greece	Given to athletes before Olympics, to soldiers before battles... *Homer, Odyssey*, 1000 BC
Ayurveda	A cure for weak digestion, abdominal pains, coughs, colds, asthma, diabetes, rheumatism, tuberculosis, hypertension, and thyroid disorders.
Unani Tibb	To treat intestinal problems, food poisoning, dysentery, asthma, and whooping cough. *Hakim Ibn Sina* *Father of Unani Tibb*, 900 BC
Chinese Medicine	As an antidote for poisons, worms, intestinal parasites... *Collection of Commentaries on the Classic of Materia Medica*, 400 AD
European Herbal Medicine	To relieve heavy mucous, chronic coughs, gas, and as a preventive against contagious diseases. *Historie of Plants, John Gerard*, 1597 AD

Garlic as Medicine — the Scientific Proof

1937	Broad spectrum antibiotic properties are demonstrated confirming Louis Pasteur's assertions.
1949	German scientists establish that allicin in garlic inhibits tumors. Subsequent studies in 1963 and 1984 confirm this.
1982	Garlic reduces stress and fatigue, improves energy levels, and acts as a tonic. *Research at Tokyo University Medical School*
1973-84	Research and survey studies in China, Italy and the US conclude that the sulphur compounds in garlic lower the risk of cancer.
1990	Garlic is used successfully to treat encephalitis and viral bronchitis. *Shanghai Second Medical University China*
1990	Garlic reduces the risk of atherosclerosis and is likely to prevent a second heart attack. *1st World Congress on the Health Significance of Garlic, Washington DC, USA*
1994	Garlic lowers blood cholesterol by inhibiting oxidation of cholesterol, thins the blood and lowers high blood pressure. *Dr Christopher Silagy & Dr Andrew Neil Oxford University*

The research continues, in laborataries and universities across the world, to learn more about the amazing healing properties of garlic...

CONTENTS

Acknowledgments

I would like to acknowledge the following contributions to this book.

For kindly granting interviews, not all of which ended up in the book, but all of which helped with my education about garlic:

Dr. Dan Bensky, Dr. Mary Bove, Dr. Hakim G. M. Chisthi, Amanda McQuade Crawford, M.N.I.M.H., Dr. Christopher Deatherage, Dr. Sonja de Graaff, Dr. Subhuti Dharmananda, Dr. David Frawley, Dr. Jane Guiltinan, Dr. Tori Hudson, Dr. Jill Stansbury, Jonathan Treasure, and Susun Weed.

For their fine books on garlic, all of which I consulted for this work: Dr. John Heinerman, Dr. Earl Mindell, Dr. Stephen Fulder, John Blackwood, and Dr. Benjamin Lau.

For research assistance: Waukanaga Corporation of America; Friedhelm Kirchfeld and Marian Frear, librarians at the National College of Naturopathic Medicine library; and the librarians of Oregon Health Sciences University.

For their Internet posts of garlic anecdotes: David Satterlee, Susan G. Wynn, DVM, and Shannon Brophy.

For editorial assistance at Prima Publishing: Leslie Yarborough and Kathryn Hashimoto.

For personal support: Mary Misel, Reyhan Beth San Juan, Mustafa Rahman Silvers, Master Ali Muhammad, Dr. Peter Overvold, Jeff Bradford, Michael Tierra, and Laura Smith.

INTRODUCTION

Is garlic a spice or a medicine? Is it therapeutic for the major diseases of our times? Scientists posed these two questions, respectively, in the titles of articles appearing in research journals in 1988. Most of us know of garlic as a favorite seasoning in salad dressings and as a staple of French, Italian, Greek, Middle Eastern, Indian, and Chinese cooking. But garlic is also a medicine, an unusually powerful and versatile one, that has been used since the dawn of medicine.

From epidemiological studies of cancer in China and Italy to clinical trials in high blood pressure and high cholesterol in the United States, Europe, and Japan, garlic has come under intense scientific scrutiny in the last ten years as a potential "wonder drug." Much of this research has investigated the effects of garlic in cardiovascular disease. This priority of research is probably inspired by the prominence of cardiovascular diseases, such as heart attack and stroke, the leading causes of death in the industrialized world.

In 1994, scientists reviewing a collection of previous clinical trials of garlic concluded that it lowers both cholesterol and blood pressure, two important risk factors for cardiovascular disease. Notably, normal dietary amounts of garlic did this without any side effects more serious than a garlic odor in a small percentage of participants. Conventional drugs for these diseases cause side effects such as dry mouth, insomnia, drowsiness, depression, and impotence. In a head-to-head trial comparing garlic against the cholesterol-lowering drug bezafibrate, garlic was just as effective. This is good news for the 25 percent of men and women aged twenty-five to fifty-nine in the United States who have high cholesterol levels.

Scientists have also recently investigated the possibility that garlic can prevent or treat some kinds of cancer. As early as 1981, scientists noted that populations in China eating more garlic had less incidence of stomach cancer than those eating less garlic. By 1985, researchers experimenting with constituents of garlic had identified mechanisms that could inhibit tumors. One focus of research has been the sulfur-containing compounds in garlic—the very compounds responsible for the odor of garlic coming from the skin of people who eat a lot of it. By 1994, the lower cancer rates among garlic eaters in China were found to also hold true in Italy and in Iowa. Scientists have now found evidence for the cancer-preventing effects of garlic from such population research, from research on isolated cancer cells, and from animal research. Cancer is the second leading cause of death in the United States, and this research suggests that garlic may help prevent stomach, bladder, breast, colon, and esophageal cancers.

So it seems that the answer to the questions posed by the scientists in 1988 is "yes." Garlic is indeed a medicine and it is a preventive for the major diseases of our times. But so far, we've only been talking about prevention. What about treatment? Garlic has been used since the dawn of written history in medicine, and its main uses have remained virtually unchanged, meaning they have been verified by one generation after another. In contemporary systems of traditional medicine, such as Chinese medicine, Ayurveda, modern naturopathic medicine, British herbalism, and others, garlic remains in use as a therapeutic agent. In 1993 and 1994, in my *Medical Herbalism* journal, I ran a survey of contemporary herbalists in North America to find out what herbs they used most often. Garlic ranked seventh out of the top fifty herbs mentioned. Note that this is not based on sales of garlic but the actual prescription of it as a medicine by clinical professionals, including naturopathic physicians, chiropractic physicians, acupuncturists, and a variety of lay herbalists. A summary of these uses shows that garlic is like a medicine chest in itself:

- Respiratory conditions:
  Cold, flu, bronchitis, asthma, pneumonia, tuberculosis
- Digestive disorders:
  Stomach ulcer, diarrhea, amoebic dysentery, worms, parasites
- Cardiovascular disease:
  Atherosclerosis, post-heart attack therapy, post-stroke therapy, claudication
- Skin problems:
  Acne, boils, eczema, fungal infections, insect bites and stings

Many of these uses come from the antibiotic and immune-stimulating effects of garlic constituents (historically, garlic was found useful even for prevention of the bubonic plague, the dreaded Black Death!). Garlic can treat or prevent many diseases caused by infection by bacteria, viruses, molds, or parasites.

In this book, I'll explain the historical and contemporary uses of garlic in detail. I'll explain how modern science understands garlic to work as a medicine. Then I'll tell you how to make more than thirty different kinds of medicinal garlic preparations and how to use them for yourself or your children in the home care of minor health complaints or in cooperation with your physician as substitutes for pharmaceutical medications. I'll help you sort out what forms of commercial garlic to use and how to find your way through the competitive advertising claims for these products. Finally, I'll thoroughly discuss the possible side effects of garlic (no medicine this powerful could be without side effects) and explain how you might overcome them if you happen to be sensitive to garlic. I'll even tell you traditional ways to overcome or adapt to the odor of garlic if that's a concern for you.

We have grown up in the era of so-called wonder drugs. Garlic seems to be perhaps the greatest wonder drug of all. Imagine a single pharmaceutical drug that could prevent heart attacks, reduce cancer risk, lower cholesterol, lower blood pressure, improve digestion, and act as an antibiotic. Each generation since before the time of the first scriptures has found garlic to be an indispensable medicine. Modern science is adding to this traditional knowledge. I hope you will learn its benefits for yourself.

Garlic in the Past

Garlic is a veritable pharmacopeia. That's why garlic has been found in every medical book of every culture ever. For thousands of years, garlic has been used for the treatment and prevention of disease. So there has to be something there.

Dr. Herbert Pierson
United States National Cancer Institute

GARLIC has been prized by human beings ever since the first records of civilization. Remains of garlic have been found in caves inhabited more than ten thousand years ago, and it is mentioned in the earliest medical records of each major civilization. Garlic has moved from nation to nation with invading armies, and strikes have been called and rebellions have been fought over it. The pyramids might not even have been completed without it! From prehistory to the present, generation after generation has cultivated garlic for its medicinal properties. It is a treasure of humanity, both as a food and as a medicine, and today even the scientific establishment, which is often skeptical about the medicinal value of nonpharmaceutical substances, has endorsed it as a medicine for a variety of serious illnesses. In this section, read about garlic in history, from the Cradle of Civilization in Mesopotamia to the twentieth century in the United States.

CHAPTER 1

HISTORY

MESOPOTAMIA

Historians call the land around the Tigris and Euphrates, in what is now Iraq and Iran, the Cradle of Civilization. It is here that the earliest written records of humanity were found, first from the Sumerian civilization and then from the Assyrians who followed. The records were inscribed on tablets of clay in cuneiform writing, an ancient alphabet of wedge shaped characters. Archaeologists have found many of these tablets, including a library from the ancient city of Nineveh. This is the same city mentioned in the Bible story of Jonah and the whale (Jonah was called to warn the residents of Nineveh that the city would be destroyed unless they changed their ways).

Many of the Nineveh tablets related the medicine of the day. The first mention of garlic appears in a recipe written in about 3000 B.C. by the Sumerians. Next, the Assyrians used garlic as a food, brewed as a tea, or mixed with wine for a variety of medicinal purposes. They ate garlic or drank it with wine as a tonic, to strengthen the system and ward off disease. They also drank garlic tea for infectious fevers and diarrhea. They applied garlic and garlic teas externally in poultices for painful swellings and for strains and sprains.

ANCIENT INDIA

From ancient India, records in the Sanskrit language document the use of garlic remedies about five thousand years ago, around the same time as the early Mesopotamian records. One of the oldest Sanskrit records in existence, the Bowers document, was copied from an older document around 350 A.D. The document suggests that garlic can cure these conditions: underweight, weak digestion, fatigue, coughs, head colds, skin problems, hemorrhoids, abdominal swelling, spleen enlargement, indigestion, abdominal pains, constipation, worms, rheumatism, tuberculosis, leprosy, and epilepsy. This list may seem excessive, but, as we'll see in the following chapters, garlic is still in use today throughout the world for many of these conditions, and modern science has verified some of these uses.

ANCIENT EGYPT

No complete ancient Egyptian herbal has survived from the days of the ancient Pharaohs, but archaeologists have gathered fragments from a variety of ancient papyrus documents to reconstruct the medicine of that time. An encyclopedia of these document fragments and their interpretations takes up nine full volumes. One of these fragments, known as the *Ebers Codex* and written in 1550 B.C., contains the first known mention of garlic in Egyptian medicine. The Codex gives twenty-two uses for garlic, including treatments for heart problems, tumors, headaches, worms, and bites.

Garlic was in use as folk medicine long before the *Ebers Codex* was written down. It was also an important element of the diet of the poor, not just as a flavoring but as a tonic to build strength and ward off disease. One Egyptian papyrus dating to 1600 B.C. describes an uprising among the men working on the pyramids because their daily food rations did not include enough garlic and onions. As we'll see later, garlic improves physical performance and protects against amebic dysentery and other epidemic diseases prevalent in Egypt.

The Holy Bible also mentions garlic as a common food in Egypt, one highly prized by the Israelites. In the Book of Numbers (11:5), the Israelites wandering in the desert lament the plain food there, saying that they miss "the fish, the cucumbers, and the melons, and the leeks, and the onions, and the garlic" that they enjoyed in Egypt.

Other documents on ancient Egyptian medicine describe its use for colds and for toothaches—infected cavities and "hollow teeth" were filled with garlic and honey to fight infection and abscess. Garlic enemas were also used for gas and indigestion. Around the time of Christ, garlic was used in Egypt for the bites of dogs and snakes. Raw garlic was a treatment for asthma. Garlic in wine was considered an aphrodisiac. Garlic oil mixed with goose fat made ear drops for earaches and to dissolve ear wax. Garlic was also mixed with salt and vinegar and used externally to treat bruises.

ANCIENT GREECE

Garlic was used throughout ancient Greece as a food and a medicine. Homer writes in his *Odyssey*, from about 1000 B.C., that garlic was part of the entertainment served by Nestor to his guest Machaon. He also says that it was garlic that allowed Ulysses to escape from Circe, who had turned his companions into pigs.

Athletes in the early Olympic games used to eat garlic before their competitions to gain strength, and Greek soldiers ate it before battle. It was used as a battlefield medicine, crushed and soaked in wine, to prevent infection in wounds. We'll see that much later it was also used in wounds during World War I in Europe for the same purpose.

Hippocrates

Hippocrates is known now as the "Father of Medicine," and the Hippocratic oath that physicians still take today is named after him. He lived in the fourth century B.C. Hippocrates laid the foundation that later would become the basis of Western medicine for about two thousand years and which remains the foundation of Arabic medicine today. Hippocrates recommended garlic for infections, wounds, cancer, leprosy, and digestive problems. He also recorded the first known cautions about side effects with garlic, saying that it "arouses wind, causes heat in the chest and heaviness in the head, can aggravate and increase existing pain, and also increases the urine."

Dioscorides

Dioscorides of Anazarba is undoubtedly the most famous Greek herbalist. He is known in both Western and

Arabic medicine as the "Father of Pharmacy." He lived in the first century A.D., after Greece had come under the rule of the Roman empire. He was a physician to the Roman army and traveled widely, recording the use of plants wherever he went. He devised a way to catalog these uses into a large work called a *materia medica* (medicinal items). This method is still used by modern pharmacists. His original work in Greek was first translated into English in 1655. The handwritten translation, written between the lines of the original Greek, took up 4,540 pages. It remained unpublished, however, until 1934.

Dioscorides' writing is characterized by a scientific objectivity, and he generally avoids editorial statement, saying that one remedy is better than another. It is notable, then, that he makes an exception to this rule for garlic, which he singles out as good for snake bites "as no other thing." We'll see later in the book that garlic is used in many cultures for toxic poisoning due to bites and stings of snakes, bees, and scorpions. He also listed the following uses for garlic, which was crushed and soaked in wine, unless otherwise noted:

- Crushed and soaked in wine to expel gas
- To treat the bites of rabid dogs to prevent hydrophobia
- To treat chronic cough
- Mixed with frankincense to treat painful teeth
- To "clear the arteries," a rather astonishing prophetic description of its modern use to treat atherosclerosis
- Crushed with black olives as a diuretic
- Mixed with salt and oil for skin afflictions
- Mixed with honey for moles and leprosy

Dioscorides, like Hippocrates, mentioned potential side effects to garlic, saying that it can injure the stomach through "dryness" and cause excessive thirst.

Ancient Rome

From ancient times the Romans ate garlic. It was a staple of the Roman army in both their food and drink. This had a practical value beyond its flavoring. Army camps were prone to epidemic diseases, and members of the army on the march could easily fall prey to dysentery or "traveler's diarrhea" much like travelers to foreign countries today. Garlic's antibiotic and immune-stimulating properties, which we'll discuss later in Chapter 8, prevented these problems. Garlic's tonic properties also gave the soldiers strength. One portable marching and battlefield food of the soldiers was a soup-like mix of boiled barley and water with crushed garlic, pomegranate, and honey. Soldiers also used poultices of moss soaked in garlic wine to disinfect battlefield wounds. They brought this use to England where it remained part of military medicine up through World War I. Roman gladiators also chewed garlic for strength before their combats, and the nobility used it as an antidote for poisoning.

Pliny the Elder

Pliny the Elder was the first Roman naturalist to write systematically about the use of garlic in Roman medicine. Pliny, a contemporary of Dioscorides, lived in the first century A.D. and produced encyclopedic writings on natural history, science, and medicine. He recorded more than sixty uses for garlic, including treatment for the common cold, asthma (raw garlic), ear problems (garlic oil), cough, worms, tuberculosis, epilepsy, and leprosy. He cautioned that garlic can dull the eyesight, cause gas, injure the stomach, and cause excessive thirst.

Galen

Undoubtedly, the greatest physician in Roman history was Galen, who reinvigorated the old Hippocratic medicine. His writings dominated Western medicine until the sixteenth century and influenced Arabic medicine for more than a thousand years. In a way, Galen owed his career to garlic. In his youth, he was physician to some gladiators in a small town. He attracted the attention of the Roman dignitaries there by devising a wound dressing that saved the lives of many wounded gladiators. He dressed their wounds, which were bleeding severely, with flour mixed with chopped garlic. He covered the dressing with a cloth, and then kept the poultice moist with garlic-infused wine. Another of his wound dressings was a mixture of garlic, myrrh, and honey. Galen also introduced the use of garlic as a disinfectant before and after surgery.

Galen called garlic *theriaca rusticorum*, "peasant's heal-all," a name which eventually reached England in the Middle Ages as Poor Man's Theriacle and into Arabia as *theriaka-al-fuqara* (theriac of the poor). In Roman times, a theriac was an antidote to serious poisoning or a treatment for a life-threatening disease. Galen, like Hippocrates and Dioscorides before him, warned of the possible irritating and drying side effects of garlic and recommended that it be cooked or boiled briefly until it lost its sharp qualities.

Garlic in the Languages of the World

Ancient Akkadian	*sûmu*
Anglo-Saxon	*garleac*
Arabic	*thum, theriaka-al-fuqara*
Babylonian	*ha-za-nu*
Bambara	*Layi*
Chinese	*dà sùan*
Czech	*cesnek kuchynsky*
Danish	*hvidlók*
English	*garlic, poor man's treacle (cure-all)*
Ancient Egyptian	*htun*
French	*ail, ail commun, perdrix de Gascogne*
German	*knoblauch, knobel*
Ancient Greek	*skorodon*
Modern Greek	*skordo*
Haitian	*Lai*
Hausa	*tatanuwa*
Hawaiian	*'Aka'Akai-Pilau*
Hindi	*lashun*
Hungarian	*fokhagyma*
Igbo	*ayo-ishi*
Italian	*agliotti, ai*
Japanese	*ninniku*
Ancient Latin	*scordium, theriaca rusticorum*
Scientific Latin	*Allium sativum*
Polish	*czosnek*
Russian	*czesnek*
Sanskrit	*aristha, lashuna*
Spanish	*ajo*
Swahili	*kitoh guu suma*
Swedish	*vitlök*
Swiss	*chnoble*
Tamil	*irulli*

The English name *garlic* comes from the Anglo-Saxon *garleac* meaning "spear-leek," describing the stem. The Latin name for garlic, used in science today, is *Allium sativum*. The source of the word *allium* is not clear, but there are several possibilities: the Latin *olere*, "to smell," the Greek *hallesthai* meaning "springing up" (describing the stem) or from the Celtic *all-brennend*, meaning "sharp taste." *Sativum* means "cultivated," reflecting the fact that this species of garlic that we know and love does not grow wild. It has, in fact, been cultivated since before written history. A measure of humanity's love for this herb is that it has spread in this cultivated form to every continent capable of growing it, with the bulbs planted by hand generation after generation since prehistory.

CHINA

Garlic has been used as a folk medicine in China since its recorded history. It first appeared in official medical texts in *Collection of Commentaries on the Classic of the Materia Medica*, in the fifth century A.D., which was among the first Chinese herbals. It was used as an antidote for poisons, for worms and intestinal parasites, for diarrhea, and for coughs. Garlic reportedly came into use in regular Chinese medicine after some peasants showed the members of a traveling emperor's court how to cure poisoning with it.

ARABIA

Garlic is called *thum* in Arabia, where it has been consumed since ancient times. At the time of the coming of the prophet Muhammad, cities in Arabia were so plagued with epidemic diseases that children were often sent as infants to wet nurses in the neighboring Bedouin tribes. The Prophet recommended to his followers that they eat garlic for its protective properties, although it is considered improper etiquette for Muslims to attend congregational prayers with garlic on their breath.

Arabic medicine supplanted the medicine of the Greeks and Romans by the eighth century A.D. and is known even today as *Unani Tibb* (medicine of the Greeks). Just as Galen developed and expanded the medicine of Hippocrates, the Arabs studied and developed the medicine of the Greeks and of Galen. The greatest physician of Arabic medicine was Hakim Ibn Sina, known in the West as Avicenna, who lived in the tenth century A.D. Avicenna's works eventually became mandatory for study in European medicine until the 1600s.

Avicenna considered garlic to be heating and drying. Garlic is still called *theriaka-al-fuqara* in Unani medicine, derived from Galen's Latin name for it. The main method of taking garlic in this system is cooking it with food. Sometimes it is boiled with milk. In general, raw garlic is considered too strong for most people's systems, although it is used externally in poultices. Unani physicians used (and still use) garlic for intestinal problems, such as food poisoning, dysentery, and other infections. It's also used for asthma, whooping cough, and ear problems.

THE HISTORICAL USES OF GARLIC

It is common when looking in old herbals to find wild and irrational claims that an herb can cure a wide variety of diseases. Often the diseases that the herb is supposedly "good for" are diseases that will get better on their own anyway, whether treated or not. Garlic is an exception. Most of the uses of garlic in this chapter are universal—they're used that way in widely divergent cultures and periods of history. Furthermore, modern science has verified that garlic has potential antibiotic, antiviral, antiartherosclerotic, blood thinning, and anticancer properties, all of which could make it useful in most of the following conditions:

> abdominal swelling, abdominal pains, arterial disease, asthma, bites (dog, snake, scorpion), boils, bronchitis, bruises, cancer, childbirth, constipation, coughs, deafness, diarrhea, digestion (weak), dysentery, earache, epilepsy, fatigue, fevers (infectious), gangrene, headaches, head colds, heart problems, hemorrhoids, high blood pressure, hoarseness, indigestion, infection, kidney problems, leprosy, plague, pneumonia, poisoning, rheumatism, skin problems, spleen enlargement, sprains, strains, toothaches, tuberculosis, tumors, ulcers (skin), underweight, whooping cough, worms, wounds

NORTHERN EUROPE

Garlic has never been as popular in northern Europe as in the Mediterranean area, nevertheless it's been used as a medicine there at least since the time of Rome. German herbalist Gerhard Madaus, author of an authoritative four-volume German scientific herbal, states that the Gauls and Germans learned of garlic's medicinal use from the Romans for seizures, and that Germans used it for that purpose for many centuries. German midwives have traditionally used it in milk to hasten labor at least since Roman times. Garlic did become more popular in Germany and Austria after the invasion of Austria by the Turks in the seventeenth century. The key event precipitating garlic's popularity was the siege of Vienna in 1683. The Turks did not take the town but underwent a long siege with a large army. For this army they had huge stocks of garlic and coffee. A force came from the north to relieve the town, and the Turks rapidly retreated, leaving behind many of their stores, including tons of coffee and garlic. These were given to the people of Vienna and thus the start of the famed Viennese coffeehouses. Garlic also became popular and is still popular in Viennese cooking.

Hildegard von Bingen

Hildegard von Bingen was a German mystic, herbalist, and music composer who lived in the eleventh century A.D. She was a renowned saint in her time. Born in 1099 in Germany, she entered a Benedictine convent as a child and became the head abbess in 1136 at the age of 37. She studied the monastic medicine of the time, by then strongly influenced by Arabic medicine, but through a series of inspirational visions she developed new uses for herbs. Her book of healing methods, which includes a *materia medica* of thirty herbs, is called *Physica*. Garlic, of course, was included among them.

In one vision, an angel appeared to her and told her that a mixture of garlic and the herb hyssop would cure asthma. The method was to make a plain tea from two garlic cloves and a handful of hyssop tops in a pot of water, simmered on low heat. The herb heal-all added to the mixture instead of hyssop would make a remedy for bloody coughs, and lavender blossoms and comfrey leaf would make a treatment for tuberculosis. These treatments were used in monasteries, which provided primary medical care at that time, until the time of Napoleon.

Paracelsus

Paracelsus was a Swiss physician who lived at the turn of the sixteenth century. He has probably been the most influential physician in the development of Western medicine after his time, and is known as the "Father of Scientific Medicine." His works also influenced the development of homeopathy as a medical science. Paracelsus was above all a practical physician, and he broke with the conventional medical dogma of his day to study widely with folk herbalists, midwives, gypsies, and other common people. He was the first of the Western physicians to suggest that garlic would protect against the bubonic plague, a use he no doubt learned from the peasants. He also noted that garlic is a remedy against poisons, is an expectorant for coughs, has diuretic properties, dispels the afterbirth (a use he learned from German midwives), and heals ulcers of the skin.

ENGLAND

Garlic was in use among the Anglo-Saxon peasants at least by the year 1000 A.D., when it was called *garleac*, or "spear-leek," to differentiate it from common leeks by the shape of its spear-like stem. Later, Geoffrey Chaucer, who wrote the *Canterbury Tales* in the fourteenth century, called garlic *theriac*, derived from the original Latin word. The two words reflect the difference between the cultures of the upper class and the peasant class in England at the time. A theriac, as noted in our discussion of Galen earlier, was an antidote against poisoning and serious, life-threatening illnesses. In English, *theriac* eventually became *theriacle,* which became *treacle,* and garlic was called "poor man's treacle" for many centuries in England.

Other theriacs or treacles in England at the time were combinations of herbs and parts of poisonous snakes. They were highly prized and often were very expensive. Sixteenth century customs records show that "treacle of Flanders" was imported by the barrel and sold at high cost in pharmacies. The name poor man's treacle, which Galen first coined in Latin some thousand years before, thus stuck in England, where the peasants could not afford the more expensive herbal remedies and relied on garlic instead.

John Gerard

The most famous of English herbals is the *Historie of Plants* by John Gerard, compiled in 1597. Gerard relied mainly on classical texts and the contemporary medical practice of his day, avoiding information from folk use. He noted that garlic "healeth the body extremely," and suggested it for a wide variety of conditions:

- For heavy mucous and for chronic coughs with mucous predominant (as opposed to dry coughs)
- For hoarseness
- With fig leaves and cumin for insect bites and bee stings
- For snake bites and other forms of poisoning
- For gas (it "breaks and consumes wind")

- From dropsy (accumulation of fluid) — "from cold"
- Boiled in milk for worms (garlic "driveth them forth")
- As a preventive against contagious diseases
- For dandruff and "scabbed heads" in children

Gerard, like major writers before him, cautioned that garlic can be overly heating for some individuals. He says it "engendereth naughty and sharp blood for such as are of that complexion."

Culpepper's Herbal

Another notable herbal in English history was written by Nicholas Culpepper a half century after Gerard's herbal. In contrast to Gerard, who was from the upper classes and who described the conventional medicine of his day, Culpepper was a man of the people who lived and worked among the poor, and whose writings were universally condemned by the medical establishment of his time. He also studied Arabic sources, which other English practitioners avoided. He was a very practical man, trained in hands-on herbalism through a pharmacy apprenticeship rather than through the book learning of the physicians.

Culpepper describes many of the same uses for garlic as Gerard with some additions, and he also offers more information on adverse side effects. In addition to the uses mentioned by Gerard, Culpepper adds these:

- Promotes menstruation (a use he may have learned either from the midwives of his time or from his studies of Arabic medicine)

- Combats lethargy and fatigue
- Protects against plague (This was well known to the peasantry of England of his day, but it was not mentioned by Gerard.)
- Useful for sores and ulcers
- Removes spots and blemishes from the skin (applied externally)
- Ripens and breaks boils and swellings
- Effective against convulsions and cramps
- Effective for hemorrhoids

Culpepper warned against excessive use of garlic, saying that for people with hot and dry constitutions it will cause great aggravation. He especially warned against its drying properties and said that people with thirst and a tendency toward dehydration should not use it.

THE PLAGUES

One of the greatest testimonies to garlic's healing powers is its reputation to prevent bubonic plague, which is caused by a bacterium spread by rodents and fleas. The airborne form of this disease, caught from sufferers whose infections have spread to their lungs, is so virulent that it kills virtually everyone who contracts it within three days. It killed hundreds of millions of people across Europe, Asia, and the Middle East during the sixth century. Another epidemic swept the same regions during the fourteenth century A.D. Known as the Black Death, it killed one-fourth to one-third the population of Europe, or about 75 million people. Small epidemics of bubonic plague continue to occur in widespread regions of the world, including the United States, but they have not spread beyond local outbreaks, partly due to rodent control and partly due to the effectiveness of modern antibiotics against the bacteria that cause it. The plague must be treated with powerful antibiotics within fifteen hours for the infected patient to survive.

There is anecdotal evidence from history that garlic can confer immunity to the Plague. The first mention of it for this use is in the writings of Paracelsus, who studied European peasant medicine in the century after the Black Death swept Europe. Historical records also show that when the plague swept the town of Chester in England in 1665, the only residents of the town that survived lived in a storehouse with a cellar full of garlic; no one living in the house died.

Perhaps the most famous instance of garlic protecting against plague occurred in Marseilles in southern France in 1721. The citizens had assigned some condemned criminals to bury the dead during an outbreak of plague, thinking that the duty would be the same as a death sentence. The thieves survived, however, and they obtained a pardon when they explained how they remained immune to infection—they drank and anointed their clothes and faces with what is now called "four thieves vinegar." The vinegar, which can still be purchased in France today, consisted of crushed garlic and some other herbs soaked in vinegar. Authorities then posted the following recipe for the peasant remedy throughout Marseilles.

Four Thieves Vinegar

Take three pints of strong white wine vinegar.

Add a handful each of wormwood, meadowsweet, wild marjoram, sage, fifty cloves of garlic, two ounces campanula roots, two ounces angelica, rosemary, and horehound, and a three-pound measure of camphor.

Place in a container for fifteen days, strain, express, then bottle.
Use by rubbing on the hands, ears, and temples from time to time and when approaching a plague victim.

The garlic and aromatic elements in the formula probably kept away fleas, whose bites can transmit plague. The ingredients are also antibiotic and immune stimulating, which could protect against contracting airborne infection from plague victims' breath.

Around this same time in England, *Bradley's Family Dictionary* reported that "to eat garlick fasting is the treacle [medicine] of the country people in the time of plague." As we'll see in Chapter 8, these are not necessarily superstitious stories. Modern science has verified that garlic is a powerful antibiotic and furthermore that it stimulates the body's natural defenses against infection.

NORTH AMERICA

The Spanish settlers of Mexico and the American Southwest brought garlic with them, for use as both food and medicine, and it is now cultivated throughout Mexico and the American Southwest. California is the largest supplier of garlic in the United States. Garlic is called *ajo* (pronounced *ah' hoe*) in Spanish. Throughout the Southwest today, it is still used in folk medicine as a cough remedy—people will eat a clove four or five times a day to clear up chronic cough with thick mucous.

Eclectic Medicine

Colonists from Britain also brought garlic with them to North America, and garlic was the main worm remedy of the early settlers. The traditional British uses were also maintained. By the mid-nineteenth century, the United States had developed a vital system of herbal medicine of its own, in the institution of the Eclectic medical profession. One of the giants of this movement was Dr. William Cook. His *Physio-Medical Dispensatory*, published in 1869, was one of the first medical-level herbal textbooks in the United States. One of the chief tasks of the medicine of the mid-nineteenth century, especially in the Midwest, was to treat illness due to overexposure to cold. Remedies called "diffusives," which would increase circulation, especially to the skin and limbs, were especially important.

Cook describes garlic as an effective stimulant and diffusive for conditions due to cold. He also listed the following properties for garlic:

- An expectorant for coughs, whether acute or chronic
- A digestive stimulant for "sluggish stomachs"
- A treatment for worms
- An emmenagogue, an herb that promotes suppressed menstruation
- The juice in the ear for deafness
- A treatment for "sudden depressions"
- An external treatment over painful joints and muscles

Like professional physicians before his time, Cook cautioned garlic's overuse or improper use, saying it can lead to overstimulation, flushed face, and headache. He said garlic should not be used internally during the existence of inflammation or acute irritation, and it should never be used for a long time. We'll learn more about side effects of garlic in Chapter 13. Cook suggested a dose of one or two cloves sliced and lightly steeped in a pint of milk, or the juice mixed with sugar for coughs.

Garlic was listed in the *United States Pharmacopoeia*, a listing of official medicines published every ten years in the United States until 1900. By the end of the 1800s, Eclectic medicine had become a major part of American medicine, and some new uses for garlic began to appear in the Eclectic literature. Cook's methods were still applied—garlic's main use remained as a medicine for coughs and worms, and the Eclectics used it widely during epidemics of pertussis, or whooping cough.

Eclectics introduced garlic's use as a counterirritant for chest complaints and especially for pneumonia. They would soak a cloth in garlic tea and apply it to the chest and back for patients with pneumonia. The irritation to the skin would promote healing circulation to the lungs, and the inhaled aromatic substances would carry garlic's antibiotic properties deep into the airways. *King's American Dispensatory*, the standard Eclectic *materia medica* from the turn of the century, states that garlic should not be used during active inflammation and that large doses can cause nausea and diarrhea in addition to other unspecified "unpleasant symptoms."

THE TWENTIETH CENTURY

Garlic has maintained its fame as a powerful healer even in the face of the rise of scientific medicine in the twentieth century.

Early in the century, the famed medical missionary Albert Schweitzer used garlic to combat amebic dysentery in Africa. During World War I, garlic poultices were used for the wounds of soldiers in Europe, much as Galen had used them nearly 2,000 years before for the gladiators in Rome. Garlic oil was diluted with water, put on swabs of sterilized moss, and applied directly to the wounds. The lives and limbs of tens of thousands of soldiers were saved in this way. Garlic was so successful at preventing infection that in 1916 the British government made a public call for tons of the bulbs, offering one shilling a pound for as much as could be produced.

By the time of the Second World War, pharmaceutical antibiotics had been discovered and were used instead of garlic. Russia, however, with tens of millions of wounded soldiers, ran out of the antibiotics, and the old World War I garlic treatment was brought back. (During the previous century, garlic had gained national fame after it saved many lives during an outbreak of a deadly influenza strain.) During the war, garlic was called Russian penicillin.

In pre-World War II Germany, garlic was used in regular medical practice as a diuretic, as an antibiotic for bladder and kidney infection, and as a treatment for malaria, chronic bronchitis, asthma, and parasites. It was also used for the first time against cancer, in this case for cancerous skin ulcers. We'll see in Chapter 10 that garlic has received extensive scientific study for its potential cancer-preventing and cancer-treating properties.

EARLY SCIENTIFIC RESEARCH

Conventional medicine in the United States started seriously developing its base in scientific research rather than clinical observation and medical tradition early in this century. "Scientific medicine" became the dominant system in the United States by the 1930s, crowding out the Eclectic, homeopathic, and other schools of medicine. Favorable studies of the clinical use of garlic began to appear right away.

- A 1918 clinical article described the use of garlic as an internal antiseptic and praised it as a remedy for diphtheria, tuberculosis, and other infectious diseases.
- Scientists experimenting with both dogs and humans discovered in 1921 that garlic tincture (garlic prepared with alcohol) caused a drop in blood pressure. They noted that blood pressure fell more in people with high blood pressure than in those with normal blood pressure.
- Experiments in 1926 demonstrated that garlic was effective for worms, a practice dating from prehistory.
- Garlic's antibiotic properties were demonstrated in 1937, just as they had been in the previous century by Louis Pasteur.

By the 1940s, when other herbal medicines had fallen from use, garlic remained the subject of scientific studies and continued to be used by some regular medical doctors for a variety of serious illnesses, even though it was no longer an official medicine in the *United States Pharmacopoeia*. Regular medical doctors continued to use it for conditions such as chronic bronchitis, asthma, and whooping cough. They also used it as an external application for arthritis. The older Eclectic practice of treating pneumonia with a poultice of bruised garlic cloves on the chest continued in the regular medical profession.

Pharmaceutical companies also continued to sell garlic preparations to medical doctors up through the late 1940s.

The Sandoz company sold Allisatin (Sandoz), an odorless and tasteless tablet preparation of garlic adsorbed on vegetable charcoal. This medicine released the garlic constituents on contact with stomach acid. It was used as an intestinal antispasmodic. The Van Patten company sold Allimin, which contained dehydrated garlic concentrate with dehydrated parsley concentrate, which was used as a vasodilator for use in high blood pressure.

SIDE EFFECTS OF GARLIC

Physicians throughout the centuries have listed the following side effects for garlic:

- Gas
- Feelings of heat
- Digestive irritation
- Heaviness in the head
- Aggravation of pain
- Increase in the flow of urine
- Dull eyesight
- Headache
- Nausea
- Flushed face

See Chapter 13 for more detail.

CONCLUSION

Garlic has been used as a medicine since the earliest days of history, in widely divergent cultures and for many of the same illnesses. That people in so many different times and places have found this plant to be a cure for so many of the same diseases is the most powerful testimony to its effectiveness. In the next section, we'll see how garlic is still used today in the major systems of natural healing in the world.

REFERENCES

Cook, William. *The Physio-Medical Dispensatory*. 1869.

Eichholz D. E., W. H. S. Jones, and H. Tackham, translators of *Pliny. Natural History*. Loeb Classical Library, 1952–1971.

Felter H. W. and J. U. Lloyd. *King's American Dispensatory*. Portland, OR: Eclectic Medical Publications, 1898.

Fulder, S. Garlic: *Nature's Original Remedy*. Rochester, VT: Healing Arts Press, 1991.

Gunther, R. T. *Greek Herbal of Dioscorides*. New York: Hafner Publishing Company, 1959.

Heinerman, J. *The Healing Benefits of Garlic: From Pharaohs to Pharmacists*. New Canaan, CT: Keats Publishing, 1994.

Madaus, G. *Lerhbuch der Bioligischen Heilmittel*. Hildesheim, Germany: Georg Olms Verlag, 1976.

Manniche, Lisa. *An Ancient Egyptian Herbal*. Austin: University of Texas Press, 1989.

Osol, A. and G. E. Farrar. *United States Dispensatory*. Philadelphia: J. B. Lippencott Company, 1947.

Strehlow, W. and G. Hertzka. *Hildegard of Bingen's Medicine*. Santa Fe, NM: Bear and Company, 1988.

von Deines, H. and H. Grapow. *Grundriss der Medizin der Alten Ägypter*. West Berlin: Westendorf, 1954–1973.

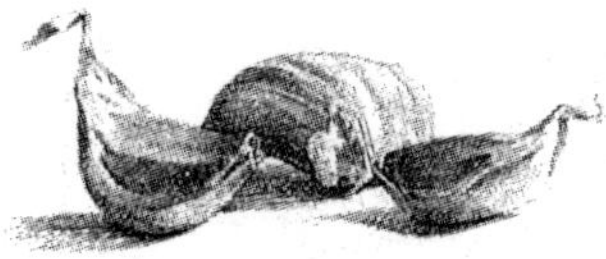

Garlic Today: Traditional and Natural Medicine

In the last chapter, we reviewed the use of garlic throughout history in different parts of the world. In this section, we'll look at garlic as it's used in the living medical traditions of the world today.

In North America, many of us have come to think of "medicine" only as conventional biomedicine. However, for much of the world, "medicine" means a traditional medical system. The World Health Organization reported several years ago that about 80 percent of the world's population uses herbal medicine in a traditional way as primary care medicine. This includes both folk medicine and formal systems of traditional medicine, such as traditional Chinese medicine, Ayurvedic medicine from India, and Unani Tibb from the Muslim world. I like to think of these systems as "parallel systems of medicine." They exist alongside conventional medicine as equals and not as inferior poor cousins. The main formal systems are Chinese, Ayurvedic, Unani Tibb, homeopathic and naturopathic medicine, traditional British herbalism, and German phytotherapy (plant medicine). We'll cover some of these systems in detail in the following chapters and see how they use garlic as a medicine.

In later chapters, I'll cover scientific research into garlic in detail. The reason I start with these traditional systems is that they probably have more practical information for the reader. Scientific biomedical research can prove something in a scholarly way, but a living tradition can usually tell you more about what to take an herb for, how much to take, what kind of patient might not tolerate an herb, and so on. These systems have been using garlic and other herbs for thousands of years and have accumulated more reliable information, in some cases, than scientific trials offer. Scientific research into garlic began, in fact, after scientists observed garlic in use in these traditional systems. We'll start our journey around the world of medicine with Chinese medicine.

CHAPTER 2

Chinese Medicine

When most Westerners hear about Chinese medicine, they first think of acupuncture. Acupuncture makes up only about 15 percent of traditional Chinese medicine, however, the rest is herbalism, dietetics, and exercises called *qi gong*. Chinese herbalism is the most developed system of herbal medicine in the world. A practitioner must study medicine for about five years. This system of herbalism has had the benefit of about 5,000 years of unbroken development, and traditional doctors today may still consult medical textbooks written 1,500 years ago. Patients may go to a formally trained practitioner, or they may self-prescribe one of thousands of herbal combinations called "patent formulas" available in pharmacies throughout the country. These are the equivalent of over-the-counter medicines in the United States but require more skill in prescribing. They can also be seen in Chinatown pharmacies throughout North America.

After the Chinese revolution, the government there first attempted to replace traditional medicine with modern biomedicine. Very soon, however, faced with the staggering problem of providing medical care to about one-fifth of the world's population, the government created an integrated system using both modern and traditional medicine. This has enriched the health care of patients in China. For example, cancer patients who receive traditional immune-stimulating herbal formulas along with chemotherapy have a higher survival rate than patients who receive chemotherapy alone. Modern Chinese medicine is a cooperative blending of this Western biomedicine, traditional herbalism and dietetics, acupuncture, and *qi gong*. Besides this official medicine, people throughout China also prescribe herbs for themselves and their families in folk traditions. The government has encouraged this and has also set up research centers throughout rural China to evaluate these folk remedies.

Garlic, called *dà sùan* in Chinese, is well known as a medicine in China, and it is used at all three levels of medicine there today, from self-care in rural villages to use by traditional herbalists, to sophisticated scientific experiments in modern hospitals.

Traditional Chinese Medicine

Dà sùan first appeared in a classical medical text, the *Collection of Commentaries on the Classic of the Materia Medica,* around 500 A.D. This was one of the earliest Chinese medical books. Garlic's use in folk medicine certainly predated this. One story is that garlic came to the attention of court physicians, and thus was introduced into traditional medicine, after peasants demonstrated to the entourage of a traveling emperor how to cure some of the court's party who had severe poisoning. Chinese herbalists have used garlic for the following conditions:

- Intestinal parasites
- Hookworm and pinworm diseases
- Ringworm on the scalp
- Poisoning
- Diarrhea and dysentery
- Tuberculosis
- Coughs
- Whooping cough
- Asthma
- Bronchitis
- Colds
- Flatulence
- Skin problems

Chinese medicine, like other traditional forms of medicine, does not treat all patients the same, even those with the same apparent illness. It evaluates the underlying energy of the patient, using concepts that do not have exact equivalents in English. A patient thus may be *hot, cold, excess,* or *deficient,* and a disease may be *exterior* or *interior.* Herbs and foods are then prescribed according to the underlying pattern. Two people may each have a cold, for instance, but one of them feels hot and is dehydrated; the other may feel chills, with heavy muscles, and have abdominal bloating. These two patients, even though they both have colds, would be treated entirely differently in traditional Chinese medicine. The hot patient would be given cooling foods and herbs, and possibly herbs to promote sweating in order to break the fever. The chilly patient, on the other hand, would be given warming herbs and foods. In this system, garlic is considered to be heating and drying. See the following chart for a description of some of the signs of heat and cold in traditional Chinese medicine.

Signs of Heat and Cold in Chinese Medicine

Use garlic with caution when there are many signs of heat, and avoid it completely with the pattern of "deficient yin."

- Signs of heat: Fast pulse, red face, hot hands and feet, craving cold foods and drinks, thirst, red tongue with yellow coat
- Signs of cold: Slow pulse, pale face, cold hands and feet, craving warm foods and drinks, pale tongue with white coat
- Signs of "deficient yin": Weakness, dizziness, spots before the eyes, thin pulse like a thread, fast pulse, night sweats, insomnia and restlessness, hot hands and feet, red face

Chinese herbalists in most cases use classical formulas hundreds or thousands of years old. These formulas typically combine four to twelve herbs, which are balanced in order to reduce side effects. Garlic does not appear in many of these formulas and is instead usually prescribed as part of the diet, with advice to either eat more of it or avoid it, depending on the energy of the patient. Another method is to take three to five cloves brewed as a tea. Garlic might also be taken raw toasted, or crushed into a paste. The Chinese consider purple-skinned garlic to work best medicinally. Chinese practitioners say that garlic is contraindicated for patients who have a syndrome they call "deficient yin." People with this condition generally feel weak and run down, and they also suffer from insomnia and restlessness, are thirsty and dehydrated, and have signs of heat, such as hot face and hands, flushed face, fast pulse, and so on. The Chinese also warn about keeping garlic in contact with the skin for too long.

MODERN RESEARCH

Chinese research centers and hospitals have done extensive clinical research into garlic. One major area of research has been dysentery and infection of the intestines causing diarrhea. Dysentery can be caused either by bacteria or by parasites, such as amoebas. These conditions are common in the countryside in China, and the cost of treating them with conventional drugs would be vast. According to the research, garlic offers a good alternative. In one trial, garlic tea (three cloves in about one-half pint of hot water, soaked for five hours) was given to patients with amebic dysentery. Eighty-eight percent of the patients recovered with the garlic alone, with an average treatment time of seven days. In a trial for bacillary dysentery, 130 patients received enemas of garlic tea. Ninety-five percent of the patients had recovered within a week.

Pinworm

In experimental treatment of pinworm with garlic, researchers gave enemas of garlic tea to 154 children aged two to nine years old. Treatments were repeated twice over the course of a week. The pinworm infection was cleared at the end of the week in 76 percent of the children.

Fungal and Yeast Infections

Chinese researchers have also investigated the clinical use of garlic against fungal and yeast infections. Twenty patients with respiratory tract fungal infections received an intravenous garlic preparation, and fourteen of the twenty showed dramatic improvement. Five more improved somewhat, and only one patient failed to respond. In another experiment, a garlic and sugar paste was given, along with multivitamins, to forty children with intestinal *Candida albicans* overgrowth. Thirty-eight of the children were cured with this method. Garlic has also been used to treat fungal meningitis, an infection of the lining of the brain.

Viral Encephalitis

Chinese garlic researchers gained world attention in 1990 at the First World Congress on the Health Significance of Garlic and Garlic Constituents. The conference, held in Washington D.C., brought together researchers from around the world and featured presentations by more than fifty scientists. Two Chinese doctors reported on more than twenty-five years of research using garlic to treat viral encephalitis. They used intravenous garlic preparations successfully to treat this life-threatening infection.

Appendicitis

Conventional doctors in China have also experimented with garlic for appendicitis. They made a paste of garlic and another herb and applied it over the appendix as an irritant, to draw healing circulation to the area. Other herbs were given internally, along with acupuncture treatments. Of 200 patients who received the treatment, 180 were resolved without the need for surgery. Note that this treatment was used only in patients with simple uncomplicated appendicitis who were also at risk for surgery due to their age or to other medical conditions. Appendicitis is not appropriate for self-diagnosis or self-treatment, and failure to get proper treatment could result in death.

Lead Poisoning

Other researchers demonstrated that raw garlic was effective in detoxifying patients with lead poisoning from industrial pollution. Patients took about two cloves of raw garlic daily.

Animal Trials

Chinese researchers have also investigated garlic or isolated garlic constituents in dozens of experiments on animals and in the test tube. They have investigated its anticancer potential (garlic in the diet was able to prevent breast cancer in mice), antiatherosclerotic effects in rabbits, antitumor effects in mice, and antibiotic effects against a wide variety of pathogenic bacteria, viruses, fungi, and parasites. Those functions haven't been proven to have clinical value, but they tend to support the traditional uses for infection.

RURAL MEDICINE

In addition to the formal body of knowledge known as Traditional Chinese medicine, folk medicine and folk herbalism are common throughout rural China. The oldest compilation of folk remedies (as opposed to the more formal medical herbalism), is *Five Two Prescriptions,* unearthed in a tomb from the Han dynasty, from the century before the birth of Christ.

The Chinese have launched many projects to spread health education and simple home remedies to rural areas in China. At one point, a small army of medical paraprofessionals called "barefoot doctors" received a minimal education in medicine—enough to practice some basic general care and to educate rural people in public health measures. They were sent out into the countryside as the primary medical caregivers and health educators there.

The information also flowed both ways. Government researchers have studied traditional folk methods and combined them with modern medical knowledge to create simple public health manuals in rural China. One such manual, from the Guangxi province in Southern China, is *Yai Yong Shu Cai*, published in 1985. It was translated into English and published under the title *Vegetables as Medicine* in 1989. Guangxi province is a mountainous area populated by many different "hill tribes." The area is rich in plants and in folk knowledge of how to use them. The Guangxi Research Institute of Traditional Chinese Medicine and Pharmacology records traditional folk uses for plants and conducts research into them. The Institute helped produce the book for the people of the region.

The following recipes are taken from that book:

- To prevent the common cold:
  Crush some garlic cloves. Obtain the juice, and dilute it with ten parts of water. These can be taken as nose drops to prevent cold or flu.
- Cough syrup for whooping cough:
  Crush about ten skinned garlic cloves. Add a cup of hot water and soak for 5–6 hours. Add sugar. Give ½ to 1 spoonful for children for coughs.

- Dysentery:
  Eat two garlic cloves raw in small amounts over the course of a day. Do this for 5–6 days.
- Boils:
  Crush some garlic and bandage it in place over the boil.

The simplicity of these remedies shows the ease with which garlic can be used as a medicine and its practical application in primary care medicine for non-lifethreatening medical conditions. We'll see more recipes from rural China in Chapters 14 and 15.

CHINESE MEDICINE IN THE UNITED STATES

Chinese medicine is practiced throughout the United States. The main centers for more than a century were the Chinatowns in the larger cities, especially on the West Coast and in New York City. Starting in the 1960s, Chinese medicine, especially acupuncture, began spreading beyond the Chinatowns. Dozens of acupuncture colleges now graduate students who are eligible for licensure as acupuncturists according to the regulations in various states. In most cases, the traditional practitioners in Chinatowns automatically receive licenses without having to go to school. The acupuncturists in the United States receive a minimal training in the use of Chinese herbs and dietetics, but most who want to use herbs regularly continue their studies beyond the basic degree.

One development that has accompanied the growth of Chinese medicine in North America is the modification of classical formulas to suit the medical complaints of modern

Americans. The classical formulas were developed for a population that was chronically exposed to extremes of heat and cold, often did not have enough to eat, and was never exposed to pollutants or pharmaceutical drugs. Americans, on the other hand, are usually sheltered from extremes of climate, eat too much instead of too little, are exposed to hundreds of pollutants in air and water, and often come to a Chinese practitioner only after taking pharmaceutical drugs for many years. In the process of revising the classical formulas, some American companies have included garlic along with traditional Chinese herbs.

Chinese Medicine and AIDS

Dr. Subhuti Dharmananda, a nationally recognized expert in Chinese herbalism, has been one of the leading authorities on altering classical Chinese formulas for use by Americans. He is also president of the Institute for Traditional Medicine in Portland, Oregon, and Director of the Immune Enhancement Project (IEP), a Portland clinic that treats about 140 AIDS patients each month. Doctors at the clinic treat the patients with acupuncture, Chinese massage, diet, and modified Chinese herbal formulas in a protocol followed in AIDS clinics in three other cities in the United States. The main herbal therapy at the clinics, however, is garlic. Dharmananda recently wrote a scientific review of garlic, entitled "Garlic as the Central Herb Therapy for AIDS." AIDS patients at the IEP are encouraged to take three to five cloves of garlic a day to prevent the secondary infections in AIDS. If they already have the infections, they take that dose three times a day. Garlic is also given in other forms, such as retention enemas and skin washes, for certain conditions. Dharmananda says that garlic probably does not effect the HIV infection itself but treats the secondary infections that cause the most serious symptoms of AIDS.

Dr. Michael Gandy

Michael Gandy is an acupuncturist who practices in Oakland, California. He was educated in the United States and Taiwan and has been practicing for more than fifteen years. He is also the author of the *Chinese Herbal Medicine Formulary* software program, a comprehensive professional-level reference to traditional Chinese formulas. "Garlic isn't used so much in the classical formulas," says Gandy, "but it's used all over the place in folk medicine." He says that he will "sneak" it into formulas sometimes. Chinese herbalists have great leeway to modify their formulas, altering the proportions of ingredients or adding or removing ingredients, depending on the needs of the patient.

Gandy uses one folk remedy for himself. He can't remember where he learned it, but he knows it's not in the regular Chinese medical texts. He uses it when he feels a cold coming on and doesn't have his needles or other herbs handy. He chops up garlic and onion with salt and vinegar, and puts them all together inside a piece of cheesecloth. He then rubs this vigorously on the inside of his arms, behind the knees, and on his chest. He says it's a great remedy, "If you don't mind stinking a little bit." This external use of garlic for potential respiratory problems is similar to treatments used for pneumonia and bronchitis in traditional Appalachian medicine in the United States and as recently as fifty years ago by conventional physicians here.

CHAPTER 3

AYURVEDIC MEDICINE

Ayurveda, the traditional medicine of India, has been around for at least three thousand years, and garlic is mentioned in the very earliest Ayurvedic records. In India, Ayurvedic doctors receive a four-year medical training, and they usually study further under advanced practitioners. Ayurveda is the primary care medical system for perhaps five hundred million people in India and Pakistan.

Ayurveda has become popularized in North America in the last ten years through the work of such doctors as Deepak Chopra, Vasant Lad, David Frawley, and Robert Svoboda. No system of licensing or regulating Ayurvedic medicine exists in the United States, some practitioners have M.D. degrees, some have no degree. Some have degrees that are not recognized in the United States. Ayurvedic services can be found in most major cities in the United States.

GARLIC IN AYURVEDA

Garlic is called *lashuna* in Sanskrit, the ancient language of Ayurvedic medicine. Ayurvedic practitioners most often use garlic as tea (the water is not boiled), a powder, juice, or a medicated oil. Ayurveda recognizes garlic's effects on the digestive, respiratory, nervous, reproductive, and circulatory systems. Garlic can also improve the general energy level, affecting the metabolism as a whole. It has been used for millennia in India as a circulatory stimulant, digestive stimulant, expectorant, antispasmodic, aphrodisiac, disinfectant, and antiworm medicine. It is also used as a powerful rejuvenative herb and detoxifier. Some of its Ayurvedic uses, in the language of Western medicine, are listed here:

> asthma, atherosclerosis, bronchial congestion, cholesterol (elevated), colds, cough, duodenal ulcers, digestion (poor), ear problems, edema, fever, flatulence, heart disease, heart palpitation, hemorrhoids, hypertension, hysteria, impotence, parasitic infections, rheumatism, skin diseases (applied externally), typhoid fever, whooping cough

GARLIC AS A TONIC

Ayurveda also uses garlic as a *tonic,* that is, a remedy to build the health in general rather than treat a particular disease. Other traditional systems also use garlic this way, and we'll see some scientific basis for it in Chapter 11. A tonic is a substance that strengthens and builds the energy of the system without depleting it. The effect is slow and steady. This is in contrast to a *stimulant,* like caffeine, that gives an initial burst of energy that is followed by depletion and depression of the system. Chinese herbs such as ginseng and licorice are tonics. Many spices, cooked in oils or *ghee* (clarified butter), are used as tonics in Ayurveda. Other spice-tonics include ginger, cardamom, cinnamon, black pepper, cloves, fennel, cumin, cayenne, and asafoetida. These herbs not only strengthen the system through gentle stimulating effects on the endocrine system, they also improve digestion and nutrition and build up the system that way.

This tonic therapy is widely incorporated into Indian cooking. A generous amount of oil is heated in a pan. The spice is then sauteed in the oil for a few minutes. Then vegetables are added and stir-fried in the oil, with the spice-infused oil coating the vegetables. Indian foods contain curry (a mixture of warming, tonic spices) not just for flavor but for the tonic properties described by Ayurveda. Tonic therapy with garlic is prescribed for people with deficient constitutions and conditions, and for vata conditions (see following). As we'll see in Chapter 4, it is also used this way throughout the Muslim civilization in the system of Unani Tibb medicine.

THE THREE DOSHAS

To understand garlic's use in Ayurvedic medicine, you'll need to learn three new terms. We all know that different human beings may have very different basic qualities. One may be by nature thin, talkative, intellectual, and restless; another is hot-tempered and active, with a sharp mind and measured speech; a third is heavyset, quiet, emotional, and steady by nature. Ayurvedic medicine pays great attention to the basic type, because each needs a different kind of diet and medicine.

Vata

The first—thin and intellectual—is the *vata* type, which is dominated by the air element and the nervous system. Air is a metaphor to describe the airy and light quality of this type. Vata types incline to disorders of the nervous and digestive system, malnourishment, wasting diseases, and any disorder with a strong nervous component. The main dietary therapy for them is to improve the quality and quantity of food. The best foods and herbs for them are calming, grounding, nurturing, and warming.

Pitta

The second—active and hot-tempered—is the *pitta* type, which is dominated by the fire element. Pitta types are prone to diseases with heat as a strong component, bleeding, high fever, and muscular, skin, blood, and circulatory system disorders. They require foods and herbs that are cooling and soothing.

Kapha

The third—heavyset and emotional—is the *kapha* type, dominated by the water element. When out of balance, this type can be sluggish and bloated and is prone to disease where phlegm and stagnation are predominant. Kapha types require a diet that is light, warm, and dry, with few mucous-producing and heavy foods.

These three types are called the three *doshas* in Ayurveda. The individual constitution is acquired at birth and remains constant throughout the life. However, a person is rarely a pure type and often is a mixture of two. Persons of one constitutional type may also have a condition characteristic of another type. Anyone who overeats heavy mucous-producing food, for instance, may acquire a kapha condition. So an Ayurvedic doctor will examine both the constitutional type and the nature of the disease before prescribing a diet or herbs. Ayurvedic doctors are as expert at diagnosis in this system as Western doctors are at basic diagnosis within the system of modern medicine.

GARLIC AND THE THREE DOSHAS

Garlic has specific effects on each of the three constitutional types. Garlic increases the fiery nature of pitta, decreases the spacy, spasmodic, and airy qualities of vata, and clears the mucous and opens the obstructed channels of the kapha type. Thus we see that although garlic is used for many conditions in Ayurveda, it is used only in two of the three doshas. This sort of refinement of garlic's use, i.e., its contraindication in people with hot dispositions, is also noted in the other traditional systems of herbalism, including traditional Chinese medicine and Unani Tibb. This may solve a mystery I hear from many people in North America: why two people with the same disease can take the same herb, and one gets better and the other gets worse.

Ayurveda cautions against garlic's side effects, especially in pitta types or conditions. It can cause hyperacidity, gastrointestinal inflammation, "hot blood," and can irritate the reproductive system, if taken by the wrong type of patient. In the following paragraphs, we'll show how garlic is used for some digestive situations and demonstrate how the three doshas are used to determine the treatment.

GARLIC AND DIGESTION IN AYURVEDA

Indigestion

Garlic is most often used for improving vata-type digestive disturbances, which include decreased digestive secretions, irregular appetite, belching or hiccuping, a sense of constriction, intestinal distention, gas, and constipation with dry, hard stools. It is contraindicated in pitta-type disorders, characterized by excess digestive secretion, heartburn, and a feeling of heat.

Diarrhea

Garlic is widely use throughout the world for diarrhea. This is mostly for diarrhea caused by infectious organisms, such as amebic dysentery; garlic has a direct antibiotic effect against them. Ayurvedic practitioners avoid the use of garlic, even in these conditions, if there are many signs of heat, such as high temperature, hot flushed face, and persistent abdominal pain.

Malabsorption

Many cases of chronic fatigue, food allergies, and candida infection are related to a malabsorption syndrome. A person may eat well, but the food is poorly digested, and not enough nutrients are assimilated in the gut. The telltale signs are undigested food in the stool, weakness and debility, poor appetite, and constipation and/or diarrhea. This condition is very typical of many Western digestive problems and probably contributes to arthritis and a number of other chronic diseases. This syndrome is universally due to vata and kapha imbalances rather than pitta, so garlic is an excellent remedy for it.

Food Allergies

Dairy and wheat allergies are very common in North America, and undiagnosed allergies are responsible for many other problems, like low energy, digestive disturbances, and emotional problems. Allergies to these two common foods are most common in kapha types. Garlic and other digestive stimulants may be helpful.

Fevers

Even fevers, which are hot by nature, can be differentiated according to the doshas. A vata fever is irregular and may rise and fall during the course of the day, accompanied by restlessness, insomnia, and pain. Kapha fevers are low-grade, with appetite loss, heaviness, fatigue, and feelings of cold. Pitta fevers have high body temperature, burning sensations, yellow tongue coat, and irritability. Garlic is a good treatment for the first two types but is contraindicated in the third.

Garlic and Yoga

Another quality of garlic in Ayurveda is that it is *tamasic.* This means that it can promote dullness or heaviness of mind. Ayurveda recognizes three actions of foods on the mind. *Sattvic* food, like grains and fruits, make the mind light and clear. *Rajasic* foods, such as coffee, make the mind agitated. The third category, tamasic, includes garlic and onions, the meat of large animals like beef and pork, old and rotten food, and some other items. The tamasic state of mind is similar to what you experience after Thanksgiving dinner when all you want to do is lie around and watch television. These food qualities are considered especially important by yogis in India, but they may not have much relevance to ordinary life. These yogis lead a sedentary life of contemplation, and most are celibate. Thus they also avoid garlic because it is a sexual stimulant. Tibetan and Zen monks, who live a similar lifestyle, also forbid garlic in their monasteries. Garlic may also aggravate the mental condition of a person who is mentally hypersensitive to psychic influences.

I practiced meditation for many years and avoided garlic strictly during that time, as was recommended by my teachers. Whenever I ate it inadvertently, I could immediately feel the dulling effect on my mind, which made contemplation more difficult. I've since found that the diet that supports this kind of lifestyle may not be grounding enough for those with practical duties, or nourishing enough for those who do physical labor. However, if you are pursuing higher consciousness through yoga or other mental disciplines, you might experiment and see if avoiding garlic helps. If you want to follow a sattvic diet, you should eliminate garlic and stimulants altogether.

AYURVEDA IN THE UNITED STATES

Dr. David Frawley is an Ayurvedic practitioner and author of two books on the subject. He is also licensed as an Oriental

Medical Doctor (O.M.D.), following studies in traditional Chinese medicine. He is president of the American Institute of Vedic Studies in Santa Fe, New Mexico.

"Garlic is almost a complete pharmacopeia in itself," says Frawley. He cites garlic's anticough, diaphoretic, mild diuretic, mucous-clearing, stimulating, grounding, and heart tonic effects as the most important properties for which he prescribes it. Frawley also appreciates that garlic is "one of the few herbs that you can get fresh." Most herbs are only available in the dried form.

"Garlic has special rejuvenative properties for the heart," Frawley states, "above and beyond its value for coronary heart disease and atherosclerosis." He sometimes prescribes it as a general heart tonic, recommending one or two cloves a day for a month or more. The dose and length of prescription depend on the individual's reaction to it, because garlic can be overheating. He considers it especially well suited to heart problems in overweight people or people with nervous dispositions, rather than in heart patients with high blood pressure, anger, and tension. These patients are of the pitta type, described previously, and garlic's stimulating and heating properties can cause them discomfort.

Frawley also thinks garlic is a good medicine for midlife crisis, due to its grounding and mental-steadying effects. He says its main adverse effects are from overheating and stimulating the sexual drive. "Of course it can also be used, along with other appropriate herbs, as an aphrodisiac, for a person with diminished sex drive." Frawley sometimes recommends garlic for vegetarians who are doing physical work and need some stronger energy. "If you want to go out and deal with aggressive people," he suggests, "you may want some garlic to back you up."

Garlic and Heart Problems in Ayurveda

Garlic is appropriate for vata- and kapha-type heart problems, but not for pitta.

- Vata-type heart disease is characterized by palpitations, insomnia, anxiety, and restlessness, and attacks may come after overwork or exercise.
- Kapha-type heart disease is congestive and obstructive, accompanying atherosclerosis and high cholesterol.
- Pitta-type heart patients show anger and irritability rather than anxiety. This is the typical movie-style heart patient, who gets angry and suddenly clutches his chest with a heart attack.

CHAPTER 4

Unani Tibb Medicine

Unani Tibb is a contemporary system of botanical medicine and dietetics based on ancient Greek and Roman medicine. As explained in Chapter 1, *Unani Tibb* means literally "the medicine of the Greeks," but Arabs and Persians developed it over the centuries, and it remains the primary care medicine throughout much of the Muslim civilization, and especially in Persia, Afghanistan, Kazakhstan, Pakistan, and India. Perhaps 200 million people use it as a primary care medical system. Unani Tibb is as elaborate as traditional Chinese or Ayurvedic medicine, but is not known as well in North America, possibly because of the lack of strong cultural ties between Muslim countries and North America and possibly because of Westerners' difficulties with the Arabic and Persian languages.

Avicenna

The pinnacle of Unani Tibb in history was the work of Persian physician Hakim Ibn Sina, known in the West as Avicenna. His five-volume *Canon of Medicine*, written in the eleventh century, is undoubtedly the most famous single medical book in history. It has served as a mandatory text not only for Muslim physicians for the last thousand years, but for European medicine as well for at least five hundred years until the 1700s. Unani Tibb was the basis of herbal medicine in central and northern Europe after the Crusades and until after the end of the Renaissance. Its basic tenets laid the foundation for natural medicine in Europe and the United States today.

ISLAM AND UNANI TIBB

Unani medicine has been profoundly influenced by the religion of Islam. The giants in Unani Tibb history were all Muslims, and its areas of influence today are predominantly Muslim. One expression of this is the avoidance of alcohol—Unani Tibb practitioners do not use alcohol tinctures or garlic in wine as we see in some other systems. One great contribution to herbal medicine that came out of this was extraction of the essential oils in herbs, called *attars* in Unani Tibb, which Persian and Arab Muslims first did through distillation of flowers and plants. This has led to an entire science of aromatherapy in Unani Tibb. We'll see later how the sayings of the prophet Muhammad have influenced the use of garlic by Muslims.

QUALITIES AND DEGREES

In Unani Tibb, as in Chinese and Ayurvedic medicine, a practitioner will assess the underlying energy of a person's constitution or illness. The main Unani principles are *hot, cold, moist,* or *dry.* As we saw in Chapter 3, in Ayurveda, the basic principles are *fiery, airy,* or *moist.* In traditional Chinese medicine, they are *hot, cold, excess,* and *deficient.* These properties don't have an exact equivalent in Western thinking but describe allegorically their main physiological effects. A person, an herb, or a food might each have any of these qualities. A moistening herb, for instance, might promote water retention or moistening of the mucous membranes, increase the oily secretions of the skin, and/or increase the ability of the blood to clot. A heating herb would speed up the metabolism, redden the complexion, and deplete the fluids. The *four humors* in this system are combinations of the above properties. The *phlegmatic* constitution is cold and moist, the *sanguine* constitution is hot and moist, the *choleric* constitution is hot and dry, and the *melancholic* constitution is cold and dry. Herbs and foods are also categorized according to the degree of such activity.

- The first degree means *unnoticed*
- The second degree means *openly*
- The third degree means *intensely* or *violently*
- The fourth degree means *completely* or *destructively*

In this system, garlic is considered hot and dry in the third degree. As such, it is used to treat conditions in people of sanguine and phlegmatic temperaments but is contraindicated in choleric temperaments and is used with caution in the melancholic patient.

USES

Garlic is called *thum* in Arabic. It is also called *theriaka-al-fuqara,* which is the Arabic equivalent of the *theriaca rusticorum* of Galen, which we discussed in Chapter 1, and which is the same as the poor man's heal-all of medieval England. Garlic is truly a heal-all in Unani Tibb. Here are some of its uses:

- Food poisoning
- Dysentery
- Intestinal infections
- Gas
- Asthma and whooping cough: we saw in Chapter 1 that it was also used for these two conditions in North America by medical doctors up through the 1930s.
- For pain "due to coldness"
- For the bites of scorpions and other animals: quick first aid for a scorpion bite, common in the desert areas of the world, is crushed garlic mixed with spittle and held directly against the bite as a poultice.
- For childhood colic: sometimes garlic boiled in a little milk, which reduces the intensity of its heating and drying properties.
- As a counterirritant for arthritis: with this technique, an irritating substance, such as garlic, is applied to the skin at the site of deeper pain, such as pain in the joints or muscles; this attracts circulation to the area and eases the pain.
- For ear problems: Tibb practitioners make ear drops from garlic oil, diluted with another carrier oil, and use it to dissolve accumulations of ear wax, a common cause of deafness; in Chapter 7, we'll see how a traditional healer from Alabama in the United States used garlic this way to cure a man's deafness.

- For corns on the feet: fresh, chopped garlic is used in a poultice or plaster.
- To promote menstruation, especially suppressed menstruation due to cold influences
- To help expel the afterbirth: midwives give garlic boiled in water or milk to the new mother.
- As an aphrodisiac for low sex drive
- As a tonic for the elderly: it is a practice from ancient times in Unani Tibb to extract garlic oil and use it as a tonic for patients bedridden with chronic illnesses. The ancient name for this is "Monk's oil" or *dihn al-ruhban*.
- Garlic consumption is usually increased when traveling to a new locality or changing one's drinking water supply, to protect against new bacteria. One practice in Unani Tibb is that root type vegetables and herbs (potatoes, onions, and garlic, in particular) are always eaten from one's own locale, since it is believed that such foods provide inoculation against local strains of viruses and bacteria.

Tibb practitioners caution against side effects with garlic, suggesting that its excessive heat can "dry up the semen," cause headache, and impair the vision.

CULPEPPER AND GARLIC

By the seventeenth century, Ibn Sina's *Canon of Medicine* had been the standard medical text in Europe for five hundred years. Nicholas Culpepper, a seventeenth-century British herbalist who studied this system, used the four humors diagnosis in his practice. He praised the virtues of garlic for a wide variety of conditions, mainly antibacterial, but he also warned:

Authors quote many other diseases this is good for; but conceal its vices. Its heat is very vehement; and all vehement hot things send up the ill-savored vapors to the brain. In choleric men it will add fuel to the fire; in men oppressed by melancholy it will attenuate the humor, and send up strong fancies, and as many strange visions to the head; therefore let it be taken internally with great moderation; outwardly you may be more bold with it.

FOOD AS MEDICINE

In Unani medicine, food is of utmost importance, and a prescription for a diet or for a change of seasoning in the diet is as likely as a prescription of a medicine. Note that many cooking spices, including garlic, are potent medicinal agents. The main method of taking garlic is with food. Hakim Chisthi, who directs the American Institute of Unani Medicine located near Ithaca, New York, says that garlic is one of the three or four basic ingredients in just about every kind of dish consumed. "Muslims probably eat more, or at least as much garlic, as anybody on earth," says Chisthi. This is at least in part due to the prophet Muhammad. It is reported that the Prophet said: "O all, eat garlic; for had it not been for the visitation of the angel of God, I would eat it myself." He also advised against the eating of garlic except when cooked. Such recommendations are considered a religious duty by devout Muslims, and thus garlic is eaten but rarely eaten raw. It is considered improper etiquette for Muslims to go to congregational prayers with the strong smell of garlic on their breath. From a practical point of view, cooking and boiling also greatly reduce garlic's irritating properties.

CRUSADER MEDICINE

An illustration of Unani medicine from the era of the Crusades shows the simplicity of this system compared to the cruder European medicine of the time. Usamah ibn-Munqidh was a Syrian nobleman born near the beginning of the twelfth century at the height of the Crusades. His memoirs, written in Arabic, are well preserved and are an important primary source of information on the history of the era. The twelfth century was the heyday of Unani Tibb, being the century following the synthesis and rejuvenation of the system by Ibn Sina.

Usamah tells the story of a woman with a mental affliction who was brought to a Muslim physician. The physician diagnosed the problem as "dryness" and modified the woman's diet, which included cutting all garlic out of it, and he "made her humor wet" with a moistening and cooling diet. In other words, he removed heating and dehydrating foods including garlic and added moistening and cooling ones. Unfortunately for the woman, a physician from the European Crusaders began to treat her and told her to eat whatever she wanted. She started eating garlic again and, predictably, the mental problems returned. The European physician diagnosed her with possession with devils and performed *trephination* on her, cutting a hole in her skull bone and putting salt into the wound. Unfortunately, the woman died. Had she continued to follow the simple recommendation of the Unani Tibb physician, she would certainly have lived longer.

HEART DISEASE

We now know today that garlic is preventive for heart disease. Hakim Chisthi studied under a Unani teacher in Afghanistan named Hakim Sharif. This man denied ever having seen or heard of anyone having a heart attack. When Chisthi described the symptoms (the person's heart stopped and he or she fell over dead), his teacher responded with disdain: "Human beings do not die that way." This story may not be so far-fetched as it sounds. Coronary heart disease was also rare in North America as recently as 1900, so much so that many doctors never saw it, and most students in teaching hospitals had to read about it in books rather than see it firsthand. It rose to be the number one killer in the United States only after work and dietary habits changed drastically and chemical pollution became commonplace. As for the Muslims in Afghanistan—could the high amounts of garlic they eat also help protect the heart and circulatory system? We'll see more about this in Chapter 9.

Chisthi has an emphatic recommendation for people taking garlic in North America: "I must say that I am at once puzzled and downright chagrined at times, to see endeavors to turn garlic into a bottled medicine. Go dig some up and eat it!"

REFERENCES

al-Sayuti. *Medicine of the Prophet S.A.S. (Tibb-ul-Nabbi) of Al-Suyuti*. Oxford, NY: Chishti Publishing Group, 1993.

Chisthi, Hakim G. M. *The Traditional Healer*. Rochester, VT: Healing Arts Press, 1988.

Chisthi, Hakim G. M. *The Book of Sufi Healing*. Rochester, VT: Healing Arts Press, 1986.

CHAPTER 5

Naturopathic Medicine

Naturopathic medicine is practiced in many forms throughout Europe and North America. In the United States and Canada, naturopathic doctors receive a four-year graduate-level education similar to a conventional medical education, except they learn therapeutic methods such as nutrition, herbalism, homeopathy, hydrotherapy, counseling, and spinal manipulation, and do not do major surgery. They learn the use of some drugs, but mostly use more natural therapies.

The term "naturopathy" was coined in the United States early in this century as a combination of *nature cure* and *homeopathy,* two systems of natural healing. Naturopaths in the New York area at the time were being persecuted by the medical profession and had to come up with a term they could use for themselves that would let them escape charges of practicing medicine without licenses. Subsequently in the United States, naturopaths were licensed in a majority of states. The profession weakened and almost fell out of existence in the 1950s, but since then it has steadily grown back. Today naturopathic doctors are licensed in ten states and four of the Canadian provinces. Four North American naturopathic colleges graduate a total of more than a hundred new doctors each year.

EUROPEAN NATURE CURE MOVEMENT

The profession grew out of the European *nature cure* movement. This healing system, dating roughly from the early 1800s in Germany, uses hydrotherapy—treatments with hot and/or cold water to stimulate the healing forces of the body—along with diet, exercise, sunbathing, and rest to restore health. It is the basis for *spa therapy* common throughout Europe, especially in eastern Europe, Germany, and France. As the nineteenth century progressed, nature cure practitioners, most of whom were unlicensed folk healers, began to use herbs and homeopathy. By the 1930s in Europe, nature cure hospitals grew up, especially in Germany. Extensive scientific research went into naturopathic methods in pre–World War II Germany and was published widely in scientific journals. The twentieth century also saw increasing study of psychology and mental healing methods to accompany the basic nature cure techniques. Many dignitaries throughout Europe and the United States, including the Archduke Ferdinand of Austria, Otto von Bismarck of Germany, Pope Leo XIII, and Franklin Delano Roosevelt, had personal naturopathic doctors, and Roosevelt credited nature cure with giving him the courage to run for president in spite of the paralysis that confined him to a wheelchair. Herbalism was introduced into the nature cure movement in the mid-nineteenth century by Father Sebastian Kneipp, a priest and folk healer, and it has been an integral part of the tradition ever since.

GARLIC AND THE NATURE CURE MOVEMENT IN FRANCE

Raymond Dextreit was a late-twentieth-century nature cure practitioner in France. In the tradition of his predecessors like Father Kneipp in Germany, he was unlicensed but had a huge public following. He wrote some forty-three books on natural healing, which have inspired and sustained the nature cure movement in France for the last generation. His methods were summarized in English for the first time in 1974 with the publication of *Our Earth Our Cure*, translated by Michael Abehsera. (The book, long out of print, was reprinted in 1995.) Dextreit's methods included water cure, diet, herbalism, and clay therapy (clay poultices and infusions).

Dextreit lists garlic as one of nature's seven marvels. His other marvels are: lemon, olive oil, sea salt, carrots, cabbage, and thyme. He lists these properties for garlic, according to his own experience:

- Kills germs and viruses, especially in the lungs
- Protects the whole organism against illness, glandular imbalance, and many other troubles. He says that garlic is used as rectal suppositories in the south of France to strengthen children's overall health.
- Dissolves the accumulations found in atherosclerosis
- Fights worms
- Prevents putrefaction in the intestines
- Purifies the blood
- Eases arthritis pains when rubbed with camphor over the sore areas

• Increases gastric secretions and the mobility of the stomach walls, and thus stimulates appetite and digestion

• Enhances the synthetic functions of the liver

• "Fluidifies" the blood. Note that Dextreit did not have the benefit of recent scientific studies showing garlic's blood-thinning properties, but knew this anyway from his experience.

• Aids (with other remedies) in the treatment and prevention of constipation, because it promotes healthy bowel bacteria

Dextreit suggests that, for internal use, garlic should be taken with food. But he says it is necessary to take garlic raw, because cooking destroys some of its medicinal properties. A healthy stomach and intestines will tolerate garlic well, he says. His recommendation of raw garlic is in contrast to the predominant use of cooked garlic that we saw in Chapter 4. I suspect that both can be correct: Unani Tibb is practiced mainly in very hot and dry climates, while Dextreit practiced in the cool and moist climate of France. Cooking garlic reduces its extreme heating and drying properties, something that might be more necessary in a hot area.

GARLIC AND NATURE CURE IN NORTH AMERICA

The nature cure and spa therapy movements were not confined to Europe. Spas that specialized in water cure methods sprang up across America in the late 1800s and early 1900s. One of the most famous was the Kellogg sanitarium at Battle Creek, Michigan. Today's Kellogg's cereal company rose out of the spa and health foods movement of a century ago. The

Seventh Day Adventists were also intimately involved with the nature cure movement, and a branch of that religion continues to make important contributions to it.

Two of the most important contemporary carriers of the nature cure tradition in the United States are Doctors Agatha and Calvin Thrash at the Yuchi Pines Institute in Seale, Alabama. The Thrashes have M.D. degrees but practice and teach natural healing methods much like their nature cure antecedents in Europe 150 years ago. The centerpiece of their methods is hydrotherapy, and they teach a system of water cure sophisticated enough to treat a wide range of serious and minor illnesses. They incorporate simple herbalism with their water and dietary treatments, and of the herbs they use, garlic is the most prominent.

In *Home Remedies: Hydrotherapy, Massage, Charcoal, and Other Simple Treatments*, the Thrashes describe their methods and suggest home treatments for seventy different conditions. A measure of how highly the Thrashes value garlic is that, of the sixteen chapters in the book, only one is devoted to herbs, and that one covers only garlic, onions, and aloe vera. They describe forty-five different conditions that garlic can be used for and explain in detail its effects as an antibiotic, antiparasitic, antifungal, digestion-promoting, and cardiovascular herb.

Chris Deatherage, N.D., is a naturopath in the tradition of the Thrashes. He and his family are Sabbatarian Anabaptists, a religious group similar to the Amish. They lead a religious life, choose farming as a lifestyle, wear clean and simple dress, refuse to enter military service, have large families, and practice natural healing as much as possible. Deatherage graduated from a four-year program at the Institute of Natural Health Science in Alabama. (The school has since closed.) He studied basic medical sciences, osteopathic manipulation, hydrotherapy, fasting, herbal medicine, and other natural healing methods. The Thrashes were on the board of the school. They lectured there from time to time, and their *Home Remedies* book was the hydrotherapy textbook for the school.

Deatherage lives and practices in rural Missouri and consults with fifty patients a week. He favors traditional nature cure in his practice, using water, fasting, diet, and herbs as his methods of choice. Garlic is one of his top medicines.

"I really like to combine garlic and hydrotherapy for acute illnesses," says Deatherage. "I find that combination works as well as anything else for conditions like pneumonia or strep throat." He often combines garlic with fever therapy. He uses hot water baths to create a fever of 102 degrees in the patient for twenty-five minutes. Along with this he gives a tea of the herb echinacea and gives raw garlic blended in carrot juice. "If the patient is real sick, we'll give three cloves every two hours in four to six ounces of carrot juice," he explains. Otherwise, he gives three doses a day for a total of nine cloves. He says he has seen serious conditions, such as abscessed mastitis, a serious infection of the breast, cured with this method quickly and permanently. Note that mastitis can have serious consequences and requires consultation with a doctor, so don't attempt self-treatment.

Deatherage also combines garlic and other herbs with fasting. He recommends fasting on weak lemon water for seven to ten days, taking herbal teas as appropriate, and taking garlic in carrot juice or else alone "chewed up real well." He also regularly uses garlic to treat parasitic infections, giardia, roundworms, pinworms, scabies, colds and flu, vaginal infections, hemorrhoids, atherosclerotic diseases, and in veterinary medicine. Deatherage advocates a vegetarian diet but says: "If you insist on eating meat, at least eat garlic with every meat meal."

NATUROPATHIC MEDICINE

Over the first few decades of the twentieth century, one stream of the nature cure movement evolved into a sophisticated medical system on a par with conventional medicine and osteopathic medicine, and the Doctor of Naturopathic Medicine (N.D.) degree came into being. By the 1920s, a four-year graduate-level standard of education was in place. The quality standards rose again dramatically in the 1970s, after a slump in the profession during the 1950s and 1960s. Today, N.D.s attend accredited medical schools, take standardized national board exams, are subject to state peer review boards, sit on federal government medical panels, and enjoy the infrastructure of a mature medical profession.

Herbal Education

N.D.s receive several hundred classroom hours in botanical medicine during their four-year degree program and hundreds more hours in clinical training in this area. Their main botanical texts are the classic *The Eclectic Materia Medica, Pharmacology, and Therapeutics* written in 1922 by Harvey Felter, M.D., and *Herbal Medicine,* a translated German medical text by Rudolph Weiss, M.D. (I'll discuss Dr. Weiss's use of garlic in detail in Chapter 6.)

Felter's text is from the heyday of Eclectic medicine, which I covered briefly in Chapter 1. This medical system, which was popular in the United States from about 1840 until the 1930s, mainly used herbal medicines. Its practitioners were M.D.s. It is hard to imagine today, in the days of powerful pharmaceutical drugs and hospital-based medicine, that a group of fully qualified general practice medical doctors used mostly herbs to treat the full range of human diseases as recently as seventy years ago in the United States, but it is true. I have a set of Eclectic medical texts on my shelf, within easy reach, and it is the most detailed reference set available in the Western world for the medicinal use of Western herbs. In terms of mastery of scholarly knowledge of herbs, clinical use in a wide variety of medical conditions, diagnostic techniques specific to herbal remedies, and close clinical observation and documentation of their effects, the Eclectics have never been matched. And despite the advances in science of the last seventy years, the information is as clinically relevant today as it was then. As the Eclectic profession faded into history, the rising naturopathic medical profession adopted many of its methods, and thus Eclectic herbalism is taught in the naturopathic schools today.

Garlic in Eclectic Medicine

The Eclectics used garlic both internally and externally. Externally, it was used to stimulate circulation to the area underneath it. It was applied as a poultice to the chest, abdomen, and sometimes over the throat in acute respiratory and abdominal afflictions. Before trying this yourself, be sure to see the cautions accompanying the directions for a poultice in Chapter 14. Applied over the bladder, it was used to promote suppressed urination. Garlic compresses were also used for tumors on the skin, basically as chemotherapy to burn them off. Garlic juice was also used in ear drops, with almond oil and glycerine.

Garlic was also applied to the feet as a poultice for brain and cerebrospinal disorders of children and for convulsions. As odd as it seems that something applied externally to the feet might affect the brain, garlic is also used this way in folk medicine in China. We'll see in Chapter 6 how a British herbalist also used this same method to treat her own case of pneumonia. Garlic foot poultices first warm the feet, attracting circulation to the area. This has a reflex reaction on the brain, constricting the circulation there. The effect is strong enough to stop a nosebleed. Garlic is also absorbed into the circulation through the feet, and its odor soon appears on the breath.

The Eclectics used garlic internally as a cough remedy and a mild diuretic. A cough syrup was made by covering crushed garlic with sugar, and then straining the liquid. This was widely used during whooping cough epidemics. Another internal use was for chronic colds. Felter also warns against using garlic when there is a high level of inflammation or irritation in the tissues. Most of these uses have passed into contemporary naturopathic medical practice.

Dr. Jill Stansbury

Dr. Jill Stansbury is Associate Professor of Botanical Medicine at National College of Naturopathic Medicine in Portland, Oregon. She also has a private practice in nearby Battleground, Washington. She teaches the following uses of garlic to sixty to eighty new students each year:

- To kill germs and viruses in bronchitis or gastrointestinal infections
- To kill yeast in systemic *candida* infections
- Combined with other lung herbs like yerba santa or coltsfoot to ease coughs
- As a diluted oil to treat ear infections
- In dietary, tincture, and/or capsule form to treat high cholesterol or blood pressure
- To treat severe athlete's foot
- Internally, along with other herbs, and as part of a skin wash, to treat acne

Stansbury teaches the use of many forms of garlic, including raw or cooked in food, as part of a tincture formula, or in commercial capsules. Some commercial naturopathic vitamin and herbal formulas also have garlic as a constituent.

Garlic and Naturopathic Gynecology

Dr. Tori Hudson also teaches at National College in Portland. She has been associate academic dean there, medical director of the teaching clinic, and currently is professor of gynecology. She is a nationally recognized expert on natural medicine for gynecology and was an advisor to the National Institutes of Health on setting up an Office of Alternative Medicine there. She has appeared several times on *Good Morning America,* which featured her gynecological research projects.

Hudson uses garlic in gynecology for vaginal yeast infections. She uses whole garlic cloves, with the skin removed, as vaginal and rectal suppositories for cases of chronic vaginal yeast infections. "You have to peel the clove, but be careful not to nick its surface," she says. Breaking the surface of a garlic clove releases irritating substances that might cause pain and blistering. She recommends this for her patients for half the day—day or night doesn't matter—and then acidophilus capsule suppositories the other half. "The gelatin capsule just melts," she explains.

Garlic and AIDS

Jane Guiltinan, N.D., is chief medical officer at the Natural Health Clinic of Bastyr University in Seattle, Washington. Bastyr University began as the John Bastyr College of Naturopathic Medicine in 1978. Over the last ten years, it has added schools of nutrition, oriental medicine, and several other disciplines, and obtained university status in 1994. Naturopathic physicians at Bastyr have conducted formal research into natural treatments of AIDS and HIV infection since 1989, and Dr. Guiltinan has been the primary clinician for the research. In 1995, Bastyr won a three-year, $840,000 National Institutes of Health grant to found the Bastyr University AIDS Research Center. The center is the leading research site for natural treatments of AIDS in the Western world.

Guiltinan suggests garlic for all her AIDS patients who can tolerate it. "I most often prescribe garlic in food form rather than capsules or extracts," says Guiltinan. "I have them eat as much as possible, either raw or cooked." At least one clinical trial has shown that garlic can improve the clinical status of AIDS patients. (See the AIDS section of Chapter 15 for more details, or see Chapter 8 for more about garlic's immune-stimulating function.)

Guiltinan says that garlic gives general immune support for AIDS patients and also helps keep the intestinal tract healthy. AIDS patients commonly get parasitic infections, and Guiltinan suggests that such infections contribute strongly to the general deterioration of health in AIDS.

Guiltinan also uses garlic for patients with worms, high cholesterol, risk of stroke, colds and flu, or sinusitis. "If people object to the smell," she says, "I try to impress on them the wonders of garlic. If a partner objects, I suggest that the partner take it too."

CHAPTER 6

Garlic in European Herbalism

Medical herbalism has a stronger presence in Europe than in America. Not only do people throughout Europe routinely treat themselves with plant medicines, but herbalists are officially recognized in some countries, and conventional physicians also sometimes prescribe herbs and *phytotherapy*, as medical-level herbalism is called in Europe—a required subject of study in medical education in some countries. In this chapter, I'll describe how the herbal professions in Britain and Germany use garlic.

British Herbalism

British herbalism as a formal profession dates to the reign of Henry VIII in the early sixteenth century. At that time, physicians, barber-surgeons, and apothecary proprietors all fought each other professionally and charged high rates for their services. During this era, the physicians organized the

Royal College of Physicians, which still exists today, and demanded regulation that would exclude the other practitioners. Henry VIII was a great fan of herbalism and took a direct interest in the preparation of his own medicines, ointments, and poultices. He issued a royal statute that criticized all the existing orthodox groups for their greed and made licensing available to herbalists. A formal licensing charter was adopted by Parliament in 1548, the year after Henry's death. An excerpt reads:

> *It shall be lawful to every person being the King's subject, having knowledge and experience of the nature of herbs, roots and waters, . . . to practice, use, and minister in and to any outward sore, uncome, wound, apostemation, outward swelling or disease, any herb or herbs, oyntments, baths, pults and amplaisters, according to their cunning, experience and knowledge in any of the diseases sores and maladies afore-said and all other like to the same . . . without suit, vexation, trouble, penalty or loss of goods.*

Today, the training of an herbalist in England includes four years or more of education with a thorough grounding in orthodox clinical medicine, including clinical diagnosis. Two schools currently have such programs. The herbal curriculum has evolved from folk traditions, physio-medicalism (a tradition from nineteenth-century North America), and modern European phytotherapy. Graduates receive a Diplomate of

Phytotherapy (Dip. Phyt.) degree. Graduates may apply for membership in the National Institute of Medical Herbalists, which maintains standards of training, practice, ethics, and research for the profession. Members use the title M.N.I.M.H. (Member of the National Institute of Medical Herbalists). To practice legally, an herbalist must be a member of the institute. About two hundred herbalists practice nationwide.

The British Herbal Medicine Association is an organization of academic and herb industry interests. Its Scientific Committee collects herbal research and publishes the *British Herbal Pharmacopoeia*, which identifies the herbs accepted for practitioners according to the 1968 Medicines Act, the law that presently recognizes herbalists. The *Pharmacopoeia* provides practitioners and regulators with the standard identification, quality standards, therapeutic uses, contraindications, and dosages for nearly two hundred and fifty herbs.

Garlic in the *Pharmacopoeia*

The *Pharmacopoeia* lists a number of actions for garlic, including:

- Increases circulation to the skin and promotes sweating
- Increases the production and clearing of mucous through coughing
- Reduces intestinal and bronchial spasm
- Kills bacteria and viruses
- Stimulates the immune activities of the white blood cells

- Lowers blood pressure
- Expels worms

Despite this wide variety of actions, in actual practice in British herbalism, garlic is most used for respiratory conditions, in chronic bronchitis, chronic respiratory congestion, recurrent colds, flu, whooping cough, and asthma. It is invariably combined with other herbs, such as coltsfoot, lobelia, or echinacea. Almost all the actions listed previously are helpful in colds and coughs. Increased sweating, for instance, can help reduce fever associated with colds and flu. The increasing of mucous and the antispasmodic qualities are helpful in cough, especially chronic cough. The antibiotic and immune-stimulating activities are also very useful in these infectious diseases. This combination of actions makes garlic a much better cold, flu, or cough remedy than over-the-counter or prescription drugs available anywhere, whether in Britain or the United States.

A British Herbalist from Vermont

Dr. Mary Bove, of Brattleboro, Vermont, is one of the most highly trained herbalists in the Western world. Already a competent practicing herbalist in 1984, she moved to England to study herbalism more formally, and she obtained her membership in the National Institute of Medical Herbalists in 1988. She immediately moved to Seattle, where she spent another five years obtaining a naturopathic medical degree and a license to practice midwifery.

While studying for her institute exam in Britain, Bove had the chance to experience the healing power of garlic herself. She was eight months pregnant with her first son when she contracted pneumonia. "I was studying so hard that I ignored the fact that I didn't feel well," she said. Soon she had severe pneumonia with pleurisy, a complication that causes pain with each deep breath or cough. Her doctor gave her antibiotics, but she was hesitant to take them at her stage of pregnancy. She tried garlic treatments instead.

"I ate six to ten chopped raw garlic cloves a day," she relates, "swallowed with water or juice." She also took echinacea and thyme in a tincture and applied garlic to her feet. (We'll see how to make garlic foot poultices in Chapter 14.) She also applied poultices of ginger and garlic directly over the spot that was painful from the pleurisy. Finally, she took yarrow baths—a pint of strong yarrow tea put into the bath water. She also received osteopathic treatments called a "lymphatic pump" that promotes the circulation of lymph in the chest area.

"I was out of crisis within two days and had a full recovery in two weeks," she relates. "The doctor never had a clue that I didn't take the antibiotics." A word of caution here for readers who might want to self-treat a condition like this: Bove's condition was potentially life-threatening, and she was being continuously monitored by health professionals. Don't attempt this treatment on yourself without medical supervision. Bove subsequently has used this treatment for other patients and for herself during another bout of pneumonia while studying naturopathic medicine in Seattle.

Bove uses garlic for other respiratory problems as well, according to her British training. "Garlic is really great for the lungs, especially combined with warming aromatic herbs like thyme and hyssop," she explains. She sees a lot of children in her medical practice in Vermont, and she uses a garlic syrup for most respiratory formulas; I'll tell you how she makes her syrup in Chapter 14. For adults, she mixes the syrup with tinctures such as lobelia, hyssop, or cramp bark. For children, she uses glycerites of the herbs instead of tinctures. (A glycerite is like a tincture, but glycerine is used for a base instead of alcohol. The glycerine has a sweet flavor that children like.) She used these formulas for dozens of cases of whooping cough, which is common in Vermont each fall and winter.

David Hoffmann, M.N.I.M.H.

One of the best-known British-trained herbalists in North America is David Hoffmann, M.N.I.M.H., author of the popular *Holistic Herbal* and other books on herbalism. Hoffman currently directs a graduate-level herbal program at the California Institute for Integral Studies in San Francisco, and he offers a correspondence course in therapeutic herbalism. In *Holistic Herbal,* Hoffman points out one of the reasons that garlic is so effective for respiratory conditions: The dynamics of garlic and the lungs, he points out, is that once in the system, antimicrobial constituents of garlic are excreted through the lungs. This is responsible for the odor of garlic on the breath of people who eat a lot of it. Hoffman notes that garlic rubbed into the feet, as Dr. Bove did for her own pneumonia, will produce an odor on the breath. Elsewhere in the book, Hoffman suggests garlic mainly for its antibiotic effect, eaten raw in the diet, for a wide variety of infectious diseases.

Amanda McQuade Crawford, M.N.I.M.H.

Another British herbalist practicing in the United States is Amanda McQuade Crawford, M.N.I.M.H. Crawford has a private practice near Los Angeles, California, and she teaches at conferences in the United States and abroad. She obtained her M.N.I.M.H. degree in 1986, and for a time afterwards she ran the herbal apothecary at the Findhorn Community in Scotland. She has taught in the United States since 1988.

"Garlic is one of my most fiery healers," says Crawford, "and the most fun to recommend, especially when people have to cut some favorite food out of their previous diet." She most commonly recommends it for patients who have high blood pressure or high cholesterol. She usually recommends garlic in food rather than as a supplement or tincture. This use comes from her training in England and is mirrored in folk traditions in Scotland.

"The diet in Scotland is quite poor, with a lot of fats and starch," she explains. The people rely a great deal on fried meat, like sausages, according to Crawford, and the folk tradition is always to include garlic and onions in those dishes. "Untutored people in the field will tell you that garlic 'cuts the grease' and keeps it from clogging you up," Crawford explains. (I'll discuss the modern scientific backing for the use of garlic for cardiovascular disease in Chapter 9.)

For atherosclerosis and other cardiovascular disease, Crawford usually recommends dietary changes, herbal combinations tailored to the needs of the patient, and garlic in the diet. She feels that garlic will actually reduce the atherosclerotic deposits in the blood vessels. She prescribes it whether or not there is hardening of the arteries, and says she sees both subjective and objective signs of improvement of atherosclerosis.

Crawford relates a story of a remarkable garlic cure that she heard from her teacher, Hein Zelystra, at the School of Phytotherapy in England. A middle-aged woman had irritable bowel syndrome so severe that she was facing surgery to remove part of the large intestine. She was desperate, and Zelystra recommended a long fast on spring water and fresh garlic. She was instructed to take one clove of garlic three times a day, with water only. The woman was willing to try anything to avoid surgery and complied. She became so weak from the fast, however, that she lay in bed most of the time. Within a week her symptoms improved greatly, due probably to the rest for the digestive system and the cleansing and antiseptic effects of the garlic.

One day her grown daughter came to visit, and the mother yelled from upstairs for her to bring a clove of garlic and water. When the daughter brought the clove, the mother said "Oh, no, you silly girl, I said a whole clove, not that little piece." She had been eating an entire *bulb* of garlic three times a day for more than a week. This treatment is not recommended—that much garlic for a long time could be harmful—but at the end of three weeks she went back to the hospital, was judged to have a completely healed colon, and was taken off the list to have surgery.

German Phytotherapy

Herbal medicine is deeply rooted at all levels of medical practice in Germany. This is partly the legacy of the work of Father Kneipp, the nineteenth-century German nature cure healer I described in the Chapter 5. Kneipp introduced herbalism, which he had learned from his mother, into the already popular nature cure movement, and "Kneippism" swept Germany and influenced health movements in other parts of the world. In Germany today, most households use herbal remedies for self-care. Herbal medicines ranging from mild teas to powerful concentrated prescription-only plant extracts are sold in pharmacies throughout Germany. The *Heilpraktikero*, a licensed medical profession of natural healers, regularly prescribe herbs. Herbal medicines also contribute an important part of spa therapy. Even M.D.s prescribe them often, and phytotherapy is a required course in German medical and pharmacy schools. About 20 percent of the official "drugs" in Germany are actually herbal preparations. The German equivalent of the United States Food and Drug Administration has a special branch just to evaluate herbal medicines.

Garlic and the Heart in Germany

In her book *Medicine and Culture*, author Lynn Payer studied the differences in the practice of medicine in the United States, England, France, and Germany. She found that in the United States, antibiotics and surgery are much more likely to be used than in the other countries. In England, the bowels are more likely to be treated with laxatives. In France, the liver is the organ more often treated. In Germany, it is the heart that is mainly treated, and thus it is no surprise that garlic is mainly viewed and used as a cardiovascular herb in Germany. This is not a new development—even in pre–World War II Germany, before the many clinical trials had proved that garlic is effective for cardiovascular disorders, garlic was the top cardiovascular herb in Germany. This use apparently came into German medicine in the nineteenth century from Austrian or Bulgarian folk herbalism. Consult Tables 6.1 and 6.2 to see how garlic was

TABLE 6.1
THE LEADING USES OF GARLIC IN GERMAN MEDICAL PRACTICE IN 1938*

Atherosclerosis and hypertension	39.2%
Diseases of the stomach and intestines	36.0%
Intestinal worms	16.4%
Respiratory diseases	6.5%
Rheumatism and gout (external use)	2.6%

*(from Madaus, G. *Lerhbuch der bioligischen Heilmittel.* Hildesheim, Germany: Georg Olms Verlag, 1938. Reprinted 1976).

used in Germany before the war. Today, garlic is still used mainly for heart and cardiovascular problems in Germany. A recent edition of the *Präparate-Liste der Naturheilkunde,* a physician's publication that lists herbal, homeopathic, and other natural remedies, contains more than a dozen references to products containing garlic. They all appear in the sections of heart and circulatory system medicines.

Garlic in the Medical Schools

The "Father of German Phytotherapy" is Dr. Rudolph F. Weiss. Weiss, a medical doctor, practiced general medicine with herbs and conventional medicines for nearly fifty years, and then retired to establish the scientific journal *Zeitschrift für Phytotherapie,* dedicated to the scientific study of herbal medicines. He also wrote *Lehrbuch der Phytotherapie,* which remains the standard medical text on phytotherapy in Germany. The book is available in English under the title *Herbal Medicine.* German medical students learn the following uses for garlic from Weiss's text.

TABLE 6.2
THE FREQUENCY OF USE OF MEDICINAL PLANTS FOR ATHEROSCLEROSIS IN GERMANY IN 1938*

Plant	Frequency
Garlic (*Allium sativum*)	32.0%
European mistletoe (*Viscum album*)	24.0%
Rye (*Secale cornutum*)	11.6%
Hawthorn (*Crataegus oxycantha*)	10.8%
Leopard's bane (*Arnica montana*)	8.5%
Bladderwrack (*Fucus vesiculosus*)	3.1%
Yohimbine (*Pausinystalia yohimbe*)	2.3%
Birch (*Betula verrucosa*)	2.3%

*(from Madaus, G. *Lehrbuch der bioligischen Heilmittel.* Hildesheim, Germany: Georg Olms Verlag, 1938).

- Pinworms

  Garlic enemas and teas are given once a week to children with severe infestations. Weiss says this treatment works as well as antiworm drugs, with fewer side effects.
- Digestive disorders, such as dysentery, parasitic infections, irritable bowel syndrome, spastic conditions, dyspepsia, diarrhea, and gas
- Tonic therapy

  Low doses for the debilitated and the elderly
- Lead poisoning, especially prevention for workers in lead plants
- Cardiovascular disease, in doses of one to three cloves a day for three to six months

Weiss teaches that the full effect of garlic is based on all its constituents. No one has been able to isolate a single most important active constituent, and the whole plant should be taken as it is.

CHAPTER 7

Garlic in Contemporary Folk Medicine

Garlic is as good as ten mothers.

Traditional folk saying

In this chapter, we'll see how contemporary folk healers in a variety of cultures use garlic today. We'll see that garlic is still used in living folk traditions much as it has been used since the dawn of history, for many of the same complaints, and in the same manners and methods as those described by classical writers from Greece, Rome, India, and Arabia.

Folk medicine is herbal practice based on word-of-mouth tradition rather than on formal schooling. It is most often passed on from mother to child, and practiced by mothers in the home. It also depends on a loose network of informal but locally recognized herbal healers. According to the World Health Organization, this is the true first line of health care for most of the population in the world, especially the nonindustrial countries. A scholarly review of folk use of garlic would certainly fill a large book, so I'll touch on a few cultures from around the world, starting with the United States.

AMERICAN SOUTHWEST

Two important folk cultures in North America are in mountainous areas of northern New Mexico and Appalachia. These areas developed distinct cultures because of their relative isolation over several centuries and because of the need to develop self-reliance based on local conditions, weather, climate, terrain, plant life, and agricultural possibilities. The American Southwest has a vibrant herbal tradition. The culture where I lived in northern New Mexico is a blending of Native American, Hispanic, and the Anglo cultures. The folk medicine there, which is widely practiced, is a blending of the Native American and the Hispanic.

I ran an herb department in a food store there and regularly bought and sold local herbs for use by the local population. Sometimes I would not even know what I was buying and selling, but after several people came in wanting to know if I wanted to buy some *epazote*, and then several more people came in wanting to buy *epazote*, I decided to start carrying it. Eventually, I carried about a dozen local herbs out of a hundred or so in the store. *Epazote*, incidentally, is *Chenopodium ambrosioides*, known to Anglos as wormseed or Mexican tea. The northern New Mexico natives use it as a seasoning for beans (it reputedly prevents gas), for dispelling worms in humans or animals, and for a variety of other complaints. It is an herb of questionable safety in pregnancy and when taken in large doses or for long periods, and I generally recommend against its regular use unless you are from a culture or tradition that knows how to use it.

Garlic is widely grown as a commercial crop in the Southwest. In the Spanish language, it is known as *ajo* (pronounced ah hoe). The local people around Taos, New Mexico, where I lived use it as a cough remedy. They would eat a clove four or five times a day to clear up chronic cough with thick mucous. Herbalist Michael Moore, who currently runs the Southwest School of Botanical Medicine in Albuquerque, New Mexico, relates another cough remedy from the area. Crush fresh garlic cloves and steep for a day or two in honey. One to two teaspoons of the mixture is used for dry hacking coughs.

APPALACHIA

The people of Appalachia for centuries developed a self-reliant culture, growing, hunting, and foraging their own food and growing or gathering their own medicines from the forest. Much of the herbal knowledge was learned from Native Americans, and other traditions came with the colonists from Europe. Many colonists in fact brought medicinal plants with them, and many herbal medicines now native throughout North America were initially brought here from Europe by colonists. Today, in many parts of Appalachia, people prefer to treat their own condition, even sometimes a serious one, or go to a local herbalist or healer (as often as not a relative), rather than go to a conventional doctor or hospital.

I have often visited friends in Leslie County, Kentucky, around the town of Hyden, and I have learned something of the culture there. In the last generation, especially beginning with the War on Poverty of the sixties and seventies, the influence of the "outside world" has become prominent (including strip mining and clear-cutting of forest areas), which in many ways is harming the culture. In other ways, however, these influences are enriching Appalachian culture. The herbalism there now is a blending of older European and pioneer American traditions, Native American usage, and is now colored by herbals from around the world and by scientific studies of herbs.

Perhaps the best documentation of Appalachia herbalism was done in a series of interviews with traditional herbalist A. L. Tommie Bass from Leesburg in Cherokee County in northeast Alabama. The results of this in-depth study was published by John K. Crellin and Jane Philpott: *Herbal Medicine Past and Present* (two volumes) from Duke University Press.

Bass describes garlic as "a favorite among the old timers—black and white" who used it in poultices on the chest for pneumonia and chest colds. They would use it fried in grease, poached, or raw. Bass says he recommends using onion poultices on sores and ulcers, because garlic is too irritating.

Bass recommends garlic for earaches and deafness. He says to warm garlic juice in any vegetable oil and put it directly into the ear. The book contains excerpts from a letter of testimony about garlic ear drops: "Tommie, Uncle John said to tell you that the earache drops you sent him done a good job on his ear. For two years he was deaf in his left ear. After using the drops for two weeks, he can now hold his hand over his good ear and hear out of his once bad ear." The improvement was probably due to the removal of ear wax by the oil.

In recent years, Bass has begun to recommend garlic as a blood thinner in heart problems. We'll see more about this use in Chapter 9. This reflects a modern use coming into

Appalachia rather than an older tradition. "Nowadays I tell them it's a blood purifier, and thins the blood," he says. "It also acts on the kidneys." Bass also now recommends some newer commercial forms of garlic, describing the proprietary odorless garlic products as "tame garlic," suggesting it for high blood pressure and diabetes.

THAILAND, CHINA, FIJI

Sonja de Graaff has a Ph.D. in nutrition and practices in Southport, Connecticut, and has worked in many areas of the world. She has observed garlic in use as folk medicine in each of them. De Graaff lived in Thailand for four-and-a-half years while working for the United Nations. "We often were in uncomfortable quarters," she relates, "refugee camps and smaller villages." The chief medical concern among the refugees and U.N. workers was infection by parasites.

"I usually refuse to take all the vaccinations and malaria tablets when I travel," de Graaff states. She resorts instead to herbal and natural remedies and refers to local wisdom when she can. "The indigenous people in Thailand taught me the best way to avoid diarrhea from parasites—we ate a lot of raw garlic, mostly in food." One day she saw her housekeeper preparing a bowl with five bulbs of garlic—that's bulbs, not cloves—and de Graaff advised her that it was better to chop garlic each day rather than in advance. The housekeeper said, "This *is* for today." "They put it in everything they eat," de Graaff explains. It might be raw in salads or cooked in stir-fries. "Everything you eat in Thailand smells of garlic." De Graaff says she doesn't use it so much in the United States, partly because of the smell and partly because the risk of parasites is low. "I always take it with me when I travel, though," she explains. Her story certainly adds a new dimension to Thai cooking.

Throughout the tropics, garlic is used in folk medicine and cooking to prevent parasite infection from infested drinking water and unsanitary farming conditions, where farmers often use human waste as fertilizer. De Graaff said she saw the same kind of use in villages in China where dysentery was a potential problem. In Fiji, her housekeeper also cooked with a lot of garlic, and people also often chewed garlic raw.

AFRICA

De Graaff also spent time doing research work in Africa, in Kenya, Zimbabwe, and Malave. She also found garlic in wide use there as folk medicine, mainly as an antibiotic, in small villages everywhere.

"The people use garlic as an antibacterial agent," she explains, "even if they don't have the concept of germs in their traditions." She saw it used for sore throats, infected wounds, and boils. For boils the people would apply garlic as a poultice and also take it internally. She also saw honey put directly into wounds, and says they healed beautifully. Modern scientists have recently been examining the wound-healing properties of honey.

On one occasion, she was allowed to observe a Masai traditional healer at work in Kenya treating an infected wound. She said he crushed the garlic and explained that one had to "see the juices" before it was ready. "Even if they don't know the chemistry of garlic," she explains, "they know you activate something by crushing it." (We'll see more about garlic's antibiotic and immune-stimulating properties in Chapter 8, and more about how crushing garlic activates the antibiotic principles of garlic in Chapter 12.) After crushing the garlic, the Masai healer put it in a cloth and applied it directly to the wound. Then he applied heat. "Sometimes I got frightened when I saw this," says de Graaff. "They're not afraid to use fire." The healer would heat the compress, the wound, and the tissue around it with a smoldering stick. This is similar, although a little rougher, to a Chinese method called *moxibustion,* where heat from smoldering herbs is applied to an acupuncture point. "Sometimes they would use a hot stone," says de Graaff, "and sometimes hot water. Sometimes they would just use the heat from the healer's hands."

FRANCE

Maurice Mességue is perhaps the most famous folk healer in this century in Europe. He learned herbalism from his father in the rural province of Gascony. This part of southern France has a blending of the folk cultures of the French, Spanish, Basque, and even Moroccan peasantry. In his early life, Mességué was regarded as a charlatan, but he eventually gained fame and patronage throughout Europe. He treated tens of thousands of patients, including such notables as Winston Churchill of England, President Herriot of France, and King Farouk of Egypt.

Mességué used about forty plants in his practice, all available locally. His main methods of treatment were herbal baths. The herbs would be prepared like a tea, in large amounts, and patients would soak their hands or feet, or take a sitz bath (immersion of the hips and groin area in a shallow bath), or douche of them. Garlic appears in many of his recipes. He used it to treat allergies, arteriosclerosis, arteritis, arthritis, asthma, urinary incontinence, bronchial diseases, acne, emphysema, hypertension, liver disease, digestive disorders, and others.

BULGARIA

I'll close this section with the folk use of garlic in Bulgaria, which helped garlic enter the mainstream of European science in the mid–twentieth century. The vehicle for this transmission was the work of Vesselin Petkov of the Bulgarian Academy of Sciences. Petkov, a great admirer of the traditional herbalism of his country, has conducted scientific experiments into traditional plant medicines for more than forty years, and his scientific studies have been responsible for bringing garlic to the attention of the wider scientific community for use in heart disease and atherosclerosis.

Bulgaria has been a rich center of herbalism since the recorded history of the area. The ancient Greek naturalist Theophrastus in his *Studies of Plants* said that Bulgaria (called Thrace in those days) was the region richest in medicinal plants in the world. The Greek Dioscorides, in his influential herbal (see Chapter 1), also described a large number of plants used by the Thracians. Dioscorides' data was subsequently used by the Roman Galen several centuries later and by the Persian Avicenna around 1000 A.D. The herbal traditions of Galen and Avicenna later became disseminated throughout Europe, Arabia, Persia, and Afghanistan. Thus, there is good precedent for the folk medicine of Bulgaria to spread into wider medical traditions.

Garlic is widely used by the Bulgarian people for treating different diseases. It was in such demand during a plague of cholera in the last century that the price of garlic skyrocketed. It has been used in traditional village medicine for typhoid fever, fever of unknown origin, malaria, worms, chronic bronchitis with abundant expectoration, chronic arthritis (as external applications), and skin diseases. According to Petkov, however, "garlic was mostly used by traditional medicine, and remains in practice for prevention and treatment of atherosclerosis and hypertension [high blood pressure]."

It was these last two uses that Petkov first investigated for garlic, and he published his results in 1948, showing that garlic prevented atherosclerosis in rabbits. Subsequent research, as we'll see in Chapter 9, has shown that garlic has potent cholesterol-lowering and blood-thinning properties and indeed will prevent or treat atherosclerosis in humans as well. Almost astonishingly, Dioscorides wrote at the time of Christ that garlic was traditionally used to "clear the arteries." I can't help but wonder if he didn't learn this from the Thracians.

Petkov subsequently published almost twenty scientific studies of garlic and inspired many more. In his research, he established that garlic reduces atherosclerosis, lowers blood pressure, prevents or treats lead poisoning, has antibiotic properties, and is an effective treatment for worms. He also found that garlic in the diet promoted the growth of pigs and cows. All of these findings were inspired by the folk wisdom of the Bulgarian herbalists.

Garlic Today: Scientific Studies

In the previous chapters, I've shown how traditional and natural healers throughout the world use garlic in medical practice. They offer us rich practical experience and advice. In the next six chapters, I'll show what science has to tell us about garlic.

The rise of medical research in the Western world dates from the late nineteenth century. Research institutions became widespread by the 1920s, and the practice of conventional medicine in the United States became dominated by scientific research rather than traditions by the 1940s. Almost as soon as doctors began doing scientific research, they began investigating garlic, and such research continues in abundance today. The major areas of research are garlic's antibiotic, immune-stimulating, detoxifying, cardiovascular, anticancer, and antistress effects.

CHAPTER 8

Antibiotic and Immune-Stimulating Properties

We've seen in previous chapters that garlic is used around the world to prevent and treat infections. In the last century, scientists have examined garlic for its ability to fight bacteria, viruses, parasites, fungi, yeasts, and molds, and have found it effective against a large number of these organisms, including many that cause serious disease in humans. Researchers have also found that garlic does more than kill germs directly—it also strengthens and activates the body's own immune system. In this chapter, we'll examine these antibiotic and immune-stimulating properties.

Garlic and Antibiotic Drugs

The germ theory of disease is less than one hundred and fifty years old. Louis Pasteur demonstrated that microbes were responsible for the decomposition of foods, showed that the anthrax bacterium caused the dreaded disease of the same name, and discovered that small viruses—too small to see in his microscope—cause rabies. In the same paper where he first published these discoveries, Pasteur mentioned that garlic had antibiotic properties. Thus garlic was the first antibiotic ever used intentionally against germs, within years of this discovery. The mass production of penicillin starting in 1941 ushered in the era of antibiotic drugs, and they are among the most commonly prescribed medicines in the world today. They have saved countless lives of people with life-threatening infections like pneumonia and such dreaded diseases as syphilis and gonorrhea. Critics of antibiotics say that they are given too frequently, especially in the United States, for minor conditions or for conditions that antibiotics will not cure, such as viral infections. Unfortunately, the germ theory and antibiotics have captured the popular imagination, and patients sometimes demand an antibiotic from their doctor inappropriately.

One weakness of the germ theory is that it does not take into account the fact that all people exposed to a particular germ do not get sick. "Fertile ground" in the patient is necessary before an infection can set in. Poor diet, chronic stress, lack of exercise, and other factors can predispose a person to infection. Killing the germ will only solve half the problem. Unfortunately, antibiotics themselves can also injure the "ground." Antibiotics can have mild to severe side effects, and their overuse contributes to such diseases as candida yeast infection, chronic digestive problems, immune-system depression, and infection by drug-resistant bacteria.

Support for these critics comes from medical writer Lynn Payer. In her 1988 book, *Medicine and Culture* (see the References section of Chapter 6), she reviews differences in the medical practice in the United States, England, Germany, and France. She points out that antibiotics are used at a much greater rate in the United States than in the other countries. In Germany, in fact, doctors usually won't give antibiotics unless a patient is sick enough to be in the hospital. Antibiotics are not among the top ten pharmaceuticals in the European drug market. Even in the United States, regular criticism of the overuse of antibiotics appears in standard medical journals. Unfortunately, medical doctors continue to routinely prescribe antibiotics for such mild conditions as acne or childhood ear infections, conditions that the drugs rarely help.

In non-lifethreatening infections like the common cold, bronchitis, childhood ear infection, or nonspecific vaginal infection, and in low-grade conditions such as acne, effective natural remedies such as garlic are superior to antibiotics. Garlic not only has fewer side effects than conventional antibiotics, it has "side benefits" as well. Garlic will kill viruses as well as bacteria, it kills candida yeast instead of promoting its growth, and it stimulates rather than depresses the immune system.

Garlic as an Antibiotic

Garlic is a *broad spectrum* antibiotic. It kills a wide variety of bacteria, including both *gram positive* and *gram negative* bacteria. (These two classes of bacteria have different kinds of cell walls.) Many antibiotics are broad spectrum, but some, such as penicillin, will only kill bacteria from one or the other of these classes of bacteria. Dr. Tariq Abdullah, a prominent garlic researcher from the Akbar Clinic and Research Center in Panama City, Florida, said in the August 1987 issue of *Prevention*: "Garlic has the broadest spectrum of any antimicrobial substance that we know of—it's antibacterial, antifungal, antiparasitic, antiprotozoan and antiviral." Researchers have even found that raw garlic extracts in rats were more effective that the common antibiotic tetracycline. Table 8.1 shows the possible advantages of garlic over conventional antibiotics.

TABLE 8.1
THE BENEFITS AND POTENTIAL SIDE EFFECTS OF GARLIC TO CONVENTIONAL ANTIBIOTICS

	Garlic	Conventional Antibiotics
Immune system	stimulates	disrupts
Active against viruses	yes	no
Allergic reactions	rare	common
Candida infection	inhibits	promotes
Possible skin rash	yes	yes
Possible nausea	yes	yes
Possible sleep disturbance	yes	yes
Possible fever reaction	no	yes
Potential kidney toxicity	no	yes
Promotes resistant bacteria	no	yes
Possible life-threatening shock	no	yes
Possible nerve damage	no	yes
Possible blood disorders	no	yes

Some Bacteria, Viruses, Fungi, Mold, and Parasites Killed or Inhibited by Garlic or Its Constituents:

Acinetobacter calcoaceticus, Aspergillus flavus, Aspergillus fumigatus, Aspergillus niger, Aspergillus parasiticus, Bacillus cereus, Candida albicans, Candida lipolytica, Cryptococcus neoformans, Cryptosporidium, Debaryomyces hansenii, Escherichia coli, Hansenula anomala, Herpes simplex virus type 1, Herpes simplex virus type 2, Histoplasma capsulatum, Human cytomegalovirus (HCMV), Human immunodeficiency virus (HIV), Human rhinovirus type 2, Influenza B, Kloeckera apiculata, Lodderomyces elongisporus, Micrococcus luteus, Mycobacterium phlei, Mycobacterium tuberculosis, Paracoccidioides brasiliensis, Parainfluenza virus type 3, Pneumocystis carinii, Proteus vulgaris, Pseudomonas aeruginosa, Rhodotorula rubra, Saccharomyces cerevisiae, Salmonella typhimurium, Shigella dysenteriae, Shigella flexneri, Staphylococcus aureus, Streptococcus faecalis, Torulopsis glabrata, Toxoplasma gondii, Vaccinia virus, Vesicular stomatitis virus, Vibrio parahaemolyticus

HOW GARLIC WORKS AS AN ANTIBIOTIC

• Oral raw garlic kills infectious bacteria in the intestines directly.

• Crushed garlic in water as a douche, or a garlic clove inserted in the vagina, kills infectious organisms in the vaginal tract.

- Garlic nose drops directly kill the viruses that cause cold or flu.
- Garlic's sulfur compounds, absorbed through food, inhalation, or poultices, and then excreted through the lungs, are antibiotic to bacteria and viruses in the lungs and bronchial tract.
- Garlic juice or oil applied to athlete's foot, staph infection, or other skin infection directly kills bacteria there.

Dr. Hiromichi Sumiyoshi of the University of Texas and others argue that because garlic can cause burns and damage tissue and friendly bacteria in high doses, raw garlic can't be used as an effective antibiotic. In very high doses, taken for a long time, garlic has indeed caused anemia and injured healthy bowel flora (see Chapter 13 on the side effects of garlic). I disagree, however, that garlic is not an effective antibiotic at lower doses than those that produce serious side effects. Garlic has proven to be an effective antibiotic clinically in humans for centuries, and, as we've seen in previous chapters, it continues to be used this way today. Also, the argument is based on the premise that only the allicin component of garlic is antibiotic. Allicin in high doses is toxic to cells and is responsible for garlic burns on the skin or irritation in the gut. Other researchers have identified different antibiotic components in garlic, such as ajoene, allyl methyl thiosulfinate, and methyl allyl thiosulfinate, and diallyl trisulfide with antibiotic properties. One study found that ajoene has even stronger antibiotic properties than allicin. These other compounds do not appear to have the toxic potential that pure allicin does.

Some research also shows that garlic, at concentrations below those that injure human tissue, are still effective against some microorganisms. There is a wide difference in doses of garlic that will kill viruses and those that kill cells. In one trial, concentrations of 1.5 milligrams of garlic per milliliter of extract were necessary to begin killing cells. One-tenth this dose was toxic to influenza virus, however, and one-hundredth of that dose killed the herpes simplex virus. Allicin will kill bacteria at concentrations as low as one part allicin in 125,000 parts water. That is the equivalent of one drop of allicin in about seventeen gallons of water!

Experiments

Researchers in India, noting that garlic is traditionally used there to prevent or treat dysentery, decided to see if it worked to cure dysentery in rabbits. First they found in a lab dish that a water extract of garlic killed all four strains of bacteria that cause most cases of dysentery. They gave the same extract to rabbits infected with one of the bacteria, *Shigella flexneri.* Within an hour of taking the extracts, the rabbits' blood serum showed activity against the bacteria. This shows that garlic can impart its antibiotic properties to the blood without injuring the rabbits, who returned to good health. Chinese researchers testing the antifungal activity of garlic for cryptococcal meningitis in humans found that the cerebrospinal fluid of patients given garlic had activity against the cryptococcal yeast. Garlic was thus able to act systemically against this yeast without destroying human cells.

Resistant Bacteria

A major problem with conventional antibiotics is that they can promote the development of resistant strains of bacteria. Initially, the antibiotic kills most of the bacteria being attacked. With repeated exposure, however, those few bacteria that by chance are genetically resistant to the antibiotic begin to multiply. Eventually, a recurring infection becomes completely resistant to that antibiotic. This has created potentially serious medical problems throughout the industrial world in the 1990s. Some resistant strains of tuberculosis, for instance, have begun to create a rise in the incidence of that disease in major cities in the United States. Resistant strains of bacteria are also responsible for some recurrent ear infections. Note that patients not following medical instructions is one of the causes of the development of resistant strains. Normally, an antibiotic should be taken for a few days after the disappearance of symptoms, but patients or their parents often discontinue the drugs before the end of a full course. If you are taking an antibiotic prescription, you should follow the instructions on the label, even if the condition seems to be gone.

Garlic does not seem to produce such resistant strains, and it may be effective against strains resistant to other antibiotics. European researchers in the late 1970s tested garlic juice against a group of ten different bacteria and yeasts. They found that garlic was effective against all of them, and they also found a "complete absence of development of resistance." In the Indian study of garlic against dysentery noted previously, the researchers specifically selected four bacterial strains that were resistant to multiple antibiotics. Garlic is effective against specific bacteria that are notorious for developing resistant strains, such as staphylococcus, mycobacterium, *salmonella,* and a species of *proteus.*

Viruses

A weakness of conventional antibiotics is that they are not effective against viral infections. That's why they won't work against the common cold or flu. They also won't work against some serious viral infections like viral meningitis, viral pneumonia, or herpes infections. Garlic or its constituents will directly kill influenza, herpes, vaccinia (cowpox), vesicular stomatitis virus (responsible for cold sores), and human cytomegalovirus (a common source of secondary infection in AIDS). Garlic will also cure or improve the symptoms of a variety of viral diseases in humans or animals. In one animal study, researchers first fed a garlic extract to mice. They then introduced the flu virus into the nasal passages of the animals. Those animals that had received the garlic were protected from the flu, while the untreated animals all got sick. The researchers postulated that garlic's effect was due in part to direct antiviral effects of garlic and in part to stimulation of the immune system. We'll see more about garlic's effect on the immune system in the next section of this chapter.

Neurologists at Shanghai Second Medical University in the People's Republic of China reported to the First World Congress on the Health Significance of Garlic and its Constituents in 1990 in Washington, D.C., that they had been using garlic to treat viral encephalitis in humans for almost three decades. Viral encephalitis is infection of the brain often caused by the herpes virus. It is difficult to treat with drugs. The researchers, who gave an intravenous extract of garlic to the patients, did not present a formal clinical trial but reported on a series of twenty case histories. In some cases, they combined the garlic with the drug amphotericin B, the conventional treatment for viral encephalitis. In their report, they singled out two cases in which even large doses of amphotericin B had been ineffective but in which garlic extract worked.

In a clinical trial in Japan, patients with the common cold or viral bronchitis received garlic, and improvement in symptoms was followed. At the end of the trial, which had no control group, almost ninety percent of the participants judged the garlic to be effective in reducing symptoms. Fatigue, aching muscles, and respiratory symptoms responded the best.

Parasites, Yeasts, and Fungi

The medical missionary Albert Schweitzer brought some fame to garlic earlier this century when he used it successfully to treat amebic dysentery in his patients in equatorial Africa. Subsequent experiments have shown garlic to be effective not only against the parasitic amoebas that cause dysentery, but against other organisms such as toxoplasma, cryptosporidia, and pneumocystis, all of which cause disease in humans. Cryptosporidia and pneumocystis infections are a common problem in AIDS patients. Garlic may be a wise first-choice treatment for these conditions, because the conventional drugs used to treat them can have severe side effects.

If you ve ever had athlete's foot, you know how stubborn a fungal infection can be. A garlic wash can be very effective against fungi externally, but garlic can also treat systemic fungal infections. Researchers from the University of New Mexico demonstrated that garlic was effective both in the test tube and in animals against infection with the fungus *Cryptococcus neoformans*. Chinese researchers also have shown that garlic as an intravenous extract can be effective against cryptococcal meningitis. The blood and cerebrospinal fluid of the patients in that trial were twice as effective against the fungus as before their treatment with garlic.

GARLIC AND THE IMMUNE SYSTEM

Although garlic attacks bacteria, viruses, and other microorganisms directly, it also stimulates the body's natural defenses against these invaders. Garlic's remarkable and legendary power against infectious diseases is due to a combination of both these properties.

Twenty years ago, little was known about the immune system. Only after the onset of the AIDS epidemic did research flourish, and immunology became a major specialty in conventional medical research. We now know that the immune system is a complex interaction among cells in many parts of the body, all coordinated to protect the body from foreign invaders. Unlike other biological systems, such as the respiration, digestion, etc., the immune system is not located in any one organ system or part of the body. The brain, the blood, the liver, the bone marrow, the lymph system, the spleen, the thymus, the skin, and some endocrine glands all work together to make up the immune system.

Just as a human army has specialties within it, so does the immune system. The front line soldiers are the white blood cells. One type, the *b-lymphocytes*, are like small floating factories, cranking out poisonous chemicals, called antibodies, that will kill a specific germ. Each of these "factory cells" makes a chemical for only one specific type of germ, but once the body has been exposed to that germ, it will make as many of the cells as necessary to fight off the infection. This part of the immune system is activated in immunizations like those that children routinely receive against serious illnesses. A small amount of a particular toxin (like a deactivated polio virus, for instance) is injected into a healthy person, and that person manufactures lymphocytes that will produce antibodies against future polio infection. This mechanism also explains why you can get some diseases like measles or mumps only once. The original infection, whether through immunization or natural infection, confers *humoral immunity*, because the antibodies float around freely in the humors, an old name for blood.

Other immune cells attack invaders directly. The two most important types are *phagocytes* and *cytotoxic T-cells*. The phagocytes are like the slow-moving infantry of an army. They attack, surround, and engulf foreign bacteria, viruses, and other material, such as dead cells. They literally swallow them up and destroy them. If you took biology in high school, you probably saw amoebas in a microscope, which engulf other microorganisms in the same way that phagocytes do. Cytotoxic T-cells, also called *natural killer cells*, are like the special forces troops of the immune system. They don't engulf the invaders but attach to them and secrete poisons into them, which kill the invaders. Unlike a phagocyte, a natural killer cell can attack many invaders, one after another. They are especially important to attack cancer cells and virally-infected cells and are thus important in the body's immunity against cancer and in fighting off the HIV infection that causes AIDS.

Garlic or its constituents activate all three of these cell types. For instance, *diallyl trisulfide,* a constituent of garlic, was found to activate natural killer cells and macrophages directly and indirectly to increase B-cell activity to make antibodies. It did this in lab experiments at concentrations of as low as one microgram per ml—the equivalent of a tiny pinch of salt in about 30 gallons of water. The macrophages in this trial were then tested for their activity against cancer cells, and the diallyl-trisulfide-treated cells were more active than regular macrophages, indicating that not only their number but their activity was increased. This same effect has been reproduced in other experiments.

This effect is not limited to trials in a test tube. Dr. Tariq Abdullah had people eat two to three bulbs of garlic daily (that's bulbs, not cloves). After three weeks he placed natural killer cells from their blood in a lab dish containing a variety of cancerous tissues. The garlic-eaters' killer cells killed more than two-and-a-half times more cancer cells than killer cells from people who had not eaten garlic. Patients do not need to eat such heroic amounts to gain some benefit. An amount as small as 1.8 grams of garlic, about half a clove, results in an increase in natural killer cell activity.

Dr. Abdullah later experimented with garlic in AIDS, giving the equivalent of two cloves a day of garlic to ten patients for six weeks and the equivalent of four cloves for another six weeks. Three of the patients could not complete the trial, but of the seven who did, all showed normal natural killer cell activity by the end of the trial—activity that had been depressed at the start of the trial. The patients' opportunistic infections, chronic diarrhea, candida infection, genital herpes, and a chronic sinus infection, all improved. The patient with the chronic sinus infection had gained no relief from antibiotics during more than a year of treatment before the garlic trial.

BEST FORMS

What's the best way to take garlic as an antibiotic? Fresh raw garlic is undoubtedly the best, because heating garlic dramatically reduces its antibiotic effects. Garlic powder or deodorized garlic capsules have little or no antibiotic effect. Chinese researchers found that the antibacterial effects of garlic oil were completely destroyed after heating for twenty minutes. Other researchers found that garlic slowly loses some of its antibiotic properties in storage. Many medicinal effects remain in heated garlic tea or cooked garlic in food, but the antibiotic properties are lost. Likewise, garlic should be chopped or crushed. As we'll see in Chapter 12, cutting into a garlic clove sets off a chemical reaction that frees powerful antibiotic constituents. My favorite forms for antibiotic use are:

- Garlic-infused wine: Chop or crush garlic, cover with wine, and let it sit overnight.
- Garlic vinegar: Same as above, but use vinegar instead of wine.
- Garlic honey: Same as above, but with honey. No added water is needed. This makes a great antibiotic cough syrup.
- Garlic/carrot juice: Blend three cloves of garlic in six ounces of carrot juice. Let it sit for four to six hours.

- Garlic douche: For vaginal infections, blend three cloves of garlic in a quart of water. Let it sit four to six hours. Then apply as a douche.

We'll see a lot more about garlic forms—more than thirty of them—in Chapter 14.

CHAPTER 9

Garlic and Cardiovascular Disease

The ancient Egyptians wrote as early as 1550 B.C. that garlic is good for the heart. Dioscorides of Anazarba, author of the greatest Roman herbal, was more specific. He stated that garlic will "clear the arteries"—an astonishing remark to make almost two thousand years before the mechanisms of atherosclerosis were discovered. Folk healers in Eastern Europe have used garlic specifically for atherosclerosis for centuries. As we saw in Chapter 7, the experiments of Bulgarian scientist Vesselin Petkov, who was inspired by these folk healers, brought garlic to international attention as a cardiovascular medicine.

Even before Petkov's work, scientists and physicians in the United States and Germany used garlic preparations for atherosclerosis and high blood pressure. A United States researcher showed in 1921 that garlic tincture caused a drop in blood pressure, and that the drop was greater in those with high blood pressure than in those with normal pressure. In

1947, the Van Patten company in the United States sold Allimin for high blood pressure. It contained dehydrated garlic concentrate with dehydrated parsley concentrate. A survey of the use of herbs for arteriosclerosis in medical practice in pre–World War II Germany showed that garlic was used more than any other herb (see "The Frequency of Use of Medicinal Plants for Arteriosclerosis in Germany in 1938" in Chapter 6, Table 6.2).

CARDIOVASCULAR DISEASE

Cardiovascular diseases—heart attacks and strokes—are the leading causes of death in the Western world today. Most of these illnesses are caused by a combination of atherosclerosis, in which the blood vessels become clogged with cholesterol deposits, and high blood pressure. These allow formation of blood clots within the vessels. In a heart attack, a blood clot blocks one of the narrowed arteries supplying blood to the heart muscle, and part of the heart tissue is destroyed. In a stroke, a similar clot forms in a vessel supplying the brain, and the brain tissue is damaged due to lack of oxygen.

The process of building up of fatty deposits in the arteries, called *plaque*, is complex. An initial lesion in the vessel wall allows a foothold for the LDL (low-density lipoprotein) cholesterol to build up a deposit. The LDL cholesterol then becomes *oxidized*, a chemical process similar to rust formation on iron. Natural immune responses in the vessels to the oxidized LDL cholesterol result in the enlargement of the deposit. Once the artery is narrowed, it becomes easier for a clot to form. However, the tendency of blood to clot can vary widely. Some dietary items or drugs can *thin* the blood, reducing its tendency to clot. Aspirin does this, for instance, and that is why some doctors recommend taking aspirin every other day for people at high risk for heart attacks. Atherosclerosis is often accompanied by high blood pressure, perhaps because the process makes the vessels less elastic, building up the pressure within them.

If a scientist were to dream up the ideal drug for this number one killer of our time, that drug would need to reduce cholesterol, reduce the oxidation of cholesterol in the fatty deposits in the arteries, lower blood pressure, and thin the blood to reduce its tendency to clot. Garlic, in fact, has all four of these actions, and some of them perform the job as well as pharmaceutical drugs.

HOW GARLIC CAN PREVENT A HEART ATTACK OR STROKE

Physiological Process	The Action of Garlic
LDL cholesterol forms a deposit in the vessel wall	Garlic lowers LDL cholesterol
The LDL cholesterol is oxidized	Garlic inhibits the oxidation of cholesterol
The oxidized cholesterol forms a larger deposit	
The vessels lose elasticity and blood pressure rises	Garlic lowers blood pressure moderately
A blood clot forms in the narrowed artery and causes tissue damage in the heart or brain	Garlic thins the blood reducing its tendency to clot

GARLIC LOWERS CHOLESTEROL

Garlic burst into the mainstream of scientific medicine in 1994 with the publication of a scientific article in the *Journal of the Royal College of Physicians* in London. Many garlic trials have appeared in the scientific literature in the last twenty years, but most have been flawed from a scientific point of view and have thus failed to gain the attention of many in the medical field. The trials were poorly designed, lacked controls, or had only small numbers of participants. What occurred in 1994 is that some conventional researchers reviewed all the research with meta-analyses. They pooled the data from many trials to solve the problem of small numbers in any one trial. The researchers discarded data from uncontrolled trials and trials that did not last long enough.

The researchers, Dr. Christopher Silagy and Dr. Andrew Neil of Oxford University, found striking results. They collected data on 952 patients from sixteen trials, and they found an average of a 12 percent reduction in cholesterol, evident after one month. Best results were with trials lasting at least three months. The typical dose was the equivalent of 600 to 900 milligrams of garlic powder. Garlic powder, fresh garlic, garlic extract, or garlic oil were all used in the various trials. An earlier meta-analysis from 1993 suggested that garlic, in an amount approximating one-half to one clove per day, decreases total serum cholesterol levels by about 9 percent. Several trials (not included in the meta-analysis) note that garlic also may lower triglycerides, another blood fat, and raise HDL-cholesterol (high-density lipoprotein, the "good" cholesterol).

Cholesterol is a natural substance in the body, and it is necessary for normal health. Only when its blood level becomes elevated does it present a health risk. Normally, it is manufactured in the liver, and garlic appears to lower cholesterol by reducing its production there. In one experiment, rat liver cells were treated in a lab dish with a garlic extract. Cholesterol production dropped by as much as 87 percent. At least five compounds in garlic have been shown to lower cholesterol synthesis by the liver.

Garlic Constituents That Inhibit the Production of Cholesterol in the Liver:

- Ajoene
- Allicin
- S-allyl-cysteine
- Diallyl disulfide
- Methyl ajoene
- 2-vinyl-4H-1,3-dithiin

Garlic and Cholesterol-Lowering Drugs

Sales of cholesterol-lowering drugs have risen in the last decade to become among the top classes of drugs sold in the United States. Their use is not without controversy, however. The drugs do lower the rate of heart attacks in patients with high cholesterol who take them. However, a number of studies show that these drugs increase the overall death rate. Accidental deaths increase among people who take them, presumably because the drugs impair people's alertness and promote accidents. Thus, if you take these drugs, you may be less likely to die of a heart attack, but more likely to die of an accident—and more likely to die overall. Garlic has no such side effects, but as we've seen, it has many "side benefits," such as reducing fatigue, improving other risk factors for heart disease, and lowering blood pressure.

One double-blind clinical trial (the highest quality of scientific trial) compared garlic with a bezafibrate, a cholesterol-lowering drug in Europe. Participants took 900 milligrams of garlic powder or 600 milligrams of the drug (the standard dose). All patients were advised to follow a lowfat diet. Both garlic and the drug lowered cholesterol significantly, lowering LDL cholesterol and raising HDL cholesterol.

Taking Garlic for High Cholesterol

Don't expect overnight results if you want to lower your cholesterol with garlic. In fact, be prepared to see your cholesterol rise a little bit for the first month, and then fall after that. Researchers don't know why this happens, but Dr. Benjamin Lau of Loma Linda University Medical School in California speculates that it is because fats are initially released from the tissues or the liver into the blood stream, and then gradually eliminated.

GARLIC AS AN ANTIOXIDANT

As we saw in the last section, cholesterol alone is not the culprit in atherosclerosis. LDL cholesterol forms the plaque that blocks the arteries, but this cholesterol must be oxidized. Oxidation of fats occurs throughout the body, especially in the cell membranes, which are all composed of fats.

This oxidation is partly responsible for aging, as we'll see in Chapter 11. Oxidation is opposed by natural mechanisms within the body, and it is supported by antioxidant substances eaten in the diet. Antioxidant vitamins such as vitamins C and E, beta carotene, and the mineral selenium are all important dietary antioxidants, and diets high in these help prevent atherosclerosis.

Garlic appears to be a potent antioxidant, and this may help explain some of its beneficial properties in preventing atherosclerosis, cancer, and some other chronic diseases. See the following list of garlic constituents that reduce the oxidation of fats in the body. One clove of garlic has about the same antioxidant power in a lab dish as 15 milligrams of vitamin C or 4.5 milligrams of vitamin E. Both these doses are low compared to the minimum daily recommended intake for these vitamins, but garlic may also increase antioxidation in the body by supporting the body's natural antioxidant systems and making fats harder to oxidize.

Garlic Constituents with Antioxidant Effects:

- aliin
- diallyl heptasulfide
- diallyl hexasulfide
- diallyl pentasulfide
- diallyl tetrasulfide
- diallyl trisulfide
- S-allyl cysteine
- S-allyl mercapto cysteine
- selenium

The connection between garlic's antioxidant properties and the reduced oxidation of LDL cholesterol is not just theoretical. Several researchers have found that garlic directly reduces the oxidation of the blood fats responsible for atherosclerosis. One test found that garlic lowered the oxidation of LDL cholesterol. In another trial, researchers gave 600 milligrams (about one-fifth of a clove) of garlic powder a day to ten healthy volunteers for two weeks. Another ten people received a placebo. In this short time, blood fats did not fall in the garlic group—that usually takes four to twelve weeks. Researchers drew blood from the volunteers, however, and found that the oxidation of LDL cholesterol had been reduced by a third in the blood of volunteers who had taken garlic.

GARLIC THINS THE BLOOD

Garlic, even in moderate dietary amounts, will thin the blood, reducing its tendency to form blood clots within the arteries. This effect of garlic came dramatically to the attention of the scientific community in the mid-1970s. Researchers in India studied members of the Jain religious sect there. Some Jains abstain completely from onions and garlic, on religious grounds, while others eat large amounts of them. A third group eats a moderate amount. Otherwise, the three populations are very similar, making their situation ideal for a controlled study of garlic. The high-garlic group consumed more than a pound of onions and at least seventeen garlic cloves weekly. The blood of members in that group had less tendency to clot than the blood of the other groups, and the group that ate no garlic at all had the highest tendency to clot.

The clinical importance of this thinning was shown in a clinical trial in patients with intermittent claudication. In this condition, associated with atherosclerosis, pain in the buttocks or legs is caused by reduced blood flow due to narrowed arteries. Garlic significantly improved the maximum walking distance in patients with claudication. The authors point out that the effects started after about five weeks of administration and that they corresponded to a simultaneous thinning of the blood at that time. It appears that the thinner blood was better able to circulate through the narrowed arteries.

It appears to make little difference whether you take your garlic raw or cooked if you want its blood-thinning effects. A group of researchers studied twenty patients who already had heart disease. The patients took garlic in either raw or fried form for four weeks. Researchers measured their blood fibrinolytic activity, a measure of the tendency of the blood to form clots. Within six hours after administration, fibrinolytic activity increased—meaning less tendency to clot—by 72 percent with raw garlic and by 63 percent with cooked. These levels remained constant up to twelve hours after administration of a single dose of garlic. The levels rose steadily throughout the next four weeks of the trial, until after twenty-eight days the activity with raw garlic was 85 percent above normal and 72 percent above normal with cooked garlic.

The final word is not in on what constituents in garlic thin the blood. One constituent, ajoene, has blood-thinning capabilities similar to aspirin. However, ajoene is not present in any significant amounts in many garlic preparations, and other researchers have suggested that allicin or a close chemical relative is responsible.

GARLIC LOWERS BLOOD PRESSURE

At least seventeen clinical trials have shown that garlic can lower blood pressure. In 1994, researchers at Oxford University in England analyzed these previous trials, and they concluded that garlic could lower blood pressure only moderately. A typical drop was 7.7 points systolic pressure and 5 points diastolic pressure. This was achieved with garlic doses of 600 to 900 milligrams of garlic powder per day for twelve weeks, the equivalent of less than a third of a clove a day. Normal blood pressure is less than 140/90 points. Severe hypertension is greater than 180/115. Most hypertension cases are mild or moderate, falling between those two levels. Thus, garlic at this dose would only correct very mild hypertension.

Higher doses of garlic may be more effective, however. One trial (not included in the meta-analysis) noted blood-pressure-lowering effects, including a 16 point drop in diastolic pressure, five hours after administering 2,400 milligrams of garlic (a little less than an average clove). The patients in that trial had severe hypertension. Doses as high as ten grams per day of fresh garlic—twelve to fifteen times the dose in the Oxford study—have been given in other garlic trials (not hypertension trials) and could be even more effective. Even if garlic will not do the whole job of lowering blood pressure, it certainly has earned a place alongside other lifestyle changes affecting blood pressure: exercise; weight loss; low-fat diet; salt restriction; supplementation with calcium, magnesium, and potassium; fish oils; stress reduction; and giving up smoking, alcohol, and caffeine.

TREATING ATHEROSCLEROSIS

We've seen above that garlic can reduce the *risk factors* for atherosclerosis—cholesterol, oxidized fats, "sticky" blood, and high blood pressure. It can also effectively treat atherosclerosis itself, as the Greek Dioscorides attested two thousand years ago. This has been demonstrated in several animal trials and hinted at in two human trials. Animals fed a high cholesterol diet along with garlic have less atherosclerosis than animals fed the same diet without garlic. Onions have the same effect, but not as strong as garlic.

Claudication

Dr. R. F. Weiss of Germany states that a series of clinical trials and observations have demonstrated that garlic can sometimes completely relieve the symptoms of claudication, which I describe under "Garlic Thins the Blood" previously (see also the discussion of claudication in Chapter 15). Weiss says that garlic sometimes works for this condition even when all other treatments have failed. The leg pain in claudication is caused by narrowed arteries cutting off blood supply to the leg muscles. Initial improvement with garlic therapy appears to be due to thinning of the blood (see page 126). However, long-term improvement and complete cure, as described by Weiss, must be due to an actual healing of the narrowed arteries.

Heart Attack

Research also shows that garlic may prevent a second heart attack if you've had one already. Researchers from

India at the First World Congress on the Health Significance of Garlic and Garlic Constituents, held in 1990 in Washington, D.C., described a three-year study among 432 patients who had already suffered one heart attack. One group received daily supplements of garlic juice in milk and the other did not. The risk factors for atherosclerosis all improved in the garlic group, and after three years only half as many of the patients in the garlic group had died. The benefits of garlic increased steadily with time, suggesting that garlic was actually dissolving the atherosclerotic blockages in coronary arteries.

CHAPTER 10

GARLIC AND CANCER

The Greek physician Hippocrates recommended garlic for cancer more than two thousand years ago, but it took until the twentieth century before scientists found reasons why it might be helpful for that disease. In this chapter, we'll see how medical scientists discovered the anticancer properties of garlic, especially its value to prevent cancer.

Cancer is not a single disease. Many types and locations of cancer exist, and their characteristics and rate of growth vary widely. One food or drug may prevent or treat one kind of cancer and be ineffective against another. As we'll see later, science shows that garlic consumption may prevent cancer of the stomach and some other cancers, but that it probably doesn't prevent cancer of the lung. However, it increases the activity of the part of the immune system that directly fights tumors, so anyone at risk of cancer, or who already has cancer, might benefit from introducing garlic into the diet. Because about one in three of us will contract cancer sometime in our lifetime, all of us are at some risk.

Investigation of garlic's role in cancer is not just fringe research. High-profile institutions have been engaged in it for more than fifty years. The research is often reproduced by other teams of scientists and published in a wide variety of scientific journals. A recent review of the scientific evidence for the antitumor properties of garlic was jointly produced by the National Cancer Institute and the American Cancer Society, two conservative organizations not prone to promoting "fad" science.

The modern story of garlic and cancer became especially exciting in the last ten years when studies correlating diet and cancer in China, Italy, and the United States all found a protective effect for garlic in the diet against cancer. Prior to this, research had been done in animals, test tubes, and lab dishes, but with questionable application to humans.

EARLY RESEARCH

Researchers have been studying the anticancer properties of garlic since at least 1949, when German scientists found that the allicin in garlic inhibited tumors in mice. During this era, scientists were looking for strong chemotherapy agents to kill tumors in cancer patients. A number of studies later verified this action of allicin. In 1964, fresh garlic extract rather than isolated allicin was found to completely inhibit the development of breast cancer in a strain of mice that is especially prone to that disease. Garlic oil inhibited skin tumors in mice in a trial published in 1983. Later, garlic constituents other than allicin were shown to help. The following are some of the constituents of garlic that have been shown to inhibit various forms of cancer in animals:

- ajoene
- allicin
- allixin
- allyl mercaptan
- allyl methyl trisulfide
- diallyl disulfide
- diallyl sulfide
- diallyl trisulfide

See Chapter 12 for more information on garlic constituents. I'll explain there how the formation of many of these compounds doesn't begin until garlic is chopped or crushed. This may explain the tradition in many cultures to crush garlic and then let it sit for some time in wine, water, or vinegar. During this waiting time, allin, the main sulfur containing constituent of garlic, is transformed into this "stew" of immune-enhancing and anticancer compounds. See Chapter 14 for ways to prepare garlic to get the most out of its power.

RECENT ANIMAL STUDIES

Many experiments with garlic constituents were conducted on animals in the late 1980s, either testing resistance to cancer-causing chemicals and radiation, or testing enhanced ability to resist implanted tumors. A 1988 study found that diallyl sulfide completely prevented tumor formation in rats treated with a cancer-causing agent. Other studies found that garlic constituents effectively prevented experimentally induced cancer of the colon, skin, esophagus, and bladder.

AN OUNCE OF PREVENTION

Cancer research underwent a big shift in the 1990s. A two-decade long "war on cancer" had failed to find a cure, and cancer rates were still increasing. Deaths from heart disease were declining, and cancer was (and still is) headed toward being the number one cause of death in industrialized countries by the turn of the century. The shift was toward prevention rather than cure of cancer. It is now a scientific consensus that prevention is a priority for research. This shift in priority follows the wisdom of classical physicians of the past. The master Persian physician Avicenna, whose *Canon of Medicine* was a basic medical text from northern Germany through Spain and north Africa all the way to Afghanistan for nearly 500 years, stated: "When cancer is advanced, it will not cure." Avicenna and other physicians of the past had many dietary recommendations to prevent cancer, however, and it was along this same course that the major cancer researchers embarked. Of course, some research on prevention had been going on all along, but now the major research and funding institutions declared prevention research to be their priority.

One impetus for this shift, and one that brought garlic into the limelight, was the publication of *Diet, Lifestyle, and Mortality in China* in 1990 by Oxford and Cornell University Presses. This book contained the results of a survey of dietary habits in China from 1973–1984. Researchers followed participants in the study to see what diseases they developed. They found, among other things, that people who ate more sulfur-rich vegetables, including cabbage, broccoli, cauliflower, garlic, onions, and leeks, had the lowest risks of cancer in general.

DESIGNER FOODS PROGRAM

The following year, 1991, was the watershed for studies of garlic and cancer prevention. To begin with, the National Cancer Institute launched a five-year Designer Foods Program. The program examines foods that are suspected to prevent cancer on the basis of either traditional medicine or recent epidemiological research. Among the foods chosen are garlic, citrus fruit, linseed, licorice root, and members of the parsley family. Scientists test these foods for safety and attempt to identify what constituents in them prevent the formation of cancer cells. Finally, the program plans to develop strains of foods or types of food products that are high in the cancer-preventing compounds. According to Herbert F. Pierson, director of the program, garlic is the food with the greatest cancer-preventing potential.

EPIDEMIOLOGY FROM CHINA TO ITALY

Also in 1991, studies appeared from China and Italy showing that garlic in the diet may lower the risk of stomach cancer. Researchers from the Shadong Province Medical College in China studied the relation between diet and stomach cancer. The area was perfect for such a study, because the Gangshan area had low stomach cancer rates (3.4 per 100,000 residents), while the nearby Quixia area had one of the highest in the world (40 per 10,000). The researchers performed a dietary analysis of 564 patients with stomach cancer and 1,131 matched controls who did not have it. On investigation, it turned out that residents of the Gangshan area ate, on the average, more than half an ounce of garlic, onions, leeks, and similar vegetables every day, while residents of the Quixia area ate almost none.

Italy is one of the European countries with the highest rates of stomach cancer, accounting for 10 percent of all cancer deaths there and causing more than 14,000 deaths a year. Scientists studied the diets and other factors of people in parts of Italy to see what might predispose them to, or prevent the cancer. As the researchers did in China, they focused on areas with very high and very low incidences of the cancer. They matched patients with gastric cancer against similar people (matched for age, sex, socioeconomic status, etc.) and then compared their diets. Researchers found that consumption of fresh fruit, citrus fruit, raw vegetables, spices, garlic, olive oil, and vitamins C, E, and beta carotene were protective against gastric cancer.

A study published the next year in 1992 added evidence for garlic's cancer-preventing properties. The study reported the results of a demographic study of cancer of the larynx, the "voice box" in the throat. In this study, in Shanghai, China, during 1988–1990, two hundred people with laryngeal cancer were compared with 414 control patients who did not have the disease. Lifestyle factors were reviewed, and it was found that garlic, along with fruits (particularly citrus fruits) and dark green and yellow vegetables conferred protection against that form of cancer.

WOMEN AND CANCER IN IOWA

Research on garlic and cancer came home to the United states in 1994. Researchers at the University of Minnesota examined the relationship of diet and colon cancer in a large group of women from Iowa.

Colon cancer is a major killer in the United States. In 1991, 112,000 new cases were diagnosed and 53,000 persons died of the disease. Only about half of people diagnosed with the disease survive for five years. Some researchers estimate that up to 90 percent of colon cancer in the United States may be avoidable through dietary modification. Previous research had indicated that fruits and vegetables may be the most protective elements against colon cancer.

The Iowa women's study provided stronger scientific evidence than previous epidemiological studies. It was a prospective study, stronger than the retrospective studies in China and Italy. In a retrospective study, researchers find a group of people who already have cancer, match them by age, sex, and other factors to a group that does not have cancer, and then ask both groups about their diet. The weakness of this approach is that it relies on the memory of the participants about what they ate in the past, leaving the results open to error. A prospective study like the one in Iowa takes a group of healthy individuals and asks them about their diet initially and periodically afterwards, and then watches to see what diseases develop. Poor memory is less of a problem, because people are asked about what they are presently eating rather than what they ate in the past. In this study, a group of 41,837 women aged 55 to 69 years was selected randomly in Iowa. They returned questionnaires about their diet in 1986.

The survey questioned such things as exercise, diet, smoking, family history, and demographic information. Participants were asked to report their consumption over the previous year of 127 food items, including twenty-nine vegetables and fifteen fruits. The group was then followed to see which participants developed colon cancer. The diets of these people were compared with people who did not get cancer.

Of the fruits and vegetables consumed, none stood out as cancer-preventive except garlic. Only total intake of garlic, total intake of vegetables as a group, and intake of total dietary fiber correlated with prevention against cancer. This study, because of its better design, offers much more convincing evidence of garlic's protective effects against cancer than the previous trials. This study in humans is also much more relevant than previous animal studies, because it uses garlic in food quantities in human beings rather than injected substances in animals. The good news is also that garlic can prevent colon cancer, one of our major killers, and not just gastric cancer, which is not a major concern in the United States. Researchers noted that liberal use of garlic was previously associated with a decreased incidence of colon cancer in Japanese Hawaiians.

FROM PREVENTION TO TREATMENT

In the stages of most cancer development, first the genetic machinery of a single cell somehow goes awry. This key step may be caused by chemicals, including pollutants or even chemicals in a normal diet, by radiation, including normal radiation from sunlight, by some viruses, or by other unknown factors. This stage, called *initiation,* is the target of preventive measures against cancer. Once a cell has become malignant, it may then grow and reproduce to form a tumor. This *promotion* stage is the target of therapies against already existing cancer. A single tumor may stabilize and stop growing through its own natural cycle, but almost immediately the tumor begins shedding malignant cells, which enter the circulation and are spread throughout the body. Once in the circulation, they are attacked vigorously by the immune system. Support of this action, and also of the immune system attack on the original tumor, is the target of immune-stimulating therapies. Most of the circulating cancer cells do not cause new tumors—perhaps only one in a million—but when they become implanted in a tissue they can create new tumors at distant sites in the body. It appears from animal research that garlic is effective against cancer at all three levels: it helps prevent both tumor initiation and promotion, and it also strengthens the immune system's attack against circulating cancer cells and the original tumor.

Initiation

Garlic appears to prevent cells turning cancerous by enhancing the body's natural mechanisms for removing toxic substances. The liver eliminates toxic chemicals and other substances from the body, and garlic protects the liver itself from damage. Garlic also has a profound effect on liver detoxification enzymes, which break down toxic substances and render them harmless. Garlic's many sulfur-rich compounds appear to be responsible for this effect. Sulfur makes up about 1 percent of garlic by weight, and dozens of sulfur-containing compounds are present in garlic, especially after it has been chopped or crushed. At the cell level, these same sulfur compounds bind to sensitive areas in a cell's genetic machinery like a key in a lock. By blocking those sites, the compounds appear to prevent cancer-causing chemicals from doing their damage to the cell. There is no single anticancer constituent in garlic. Allicin, diallyl sulfide (DAS), ajoene, allixin, garlic oil, and fresh and aged garlic extracts have all exhibited some anticancer-initiation properties.

Aflatoxin is a cancer-causing mold that occurs naturally in many kinds of food. In several experiments, researchers found that garlic or its constituents inhibit the cancer-causing effects of aflatoxin Ajoene, DAS, allixin, and crude garlic extract itself have all been shown to do this, in a dose-dependent manner.

Radiation

Garlic has also protected against radiation-induced cancer. Note that a certain level of radiation is normal in the environment, coming from the sun. This is the radiation that puts sunbathers at greater risk for skin cancer. Radiation is also increasingly present in the environment due to pollution from energy or weapons production. Areas around some nuclear plants in the United States have higher cancer rates. Wide areas downwind from the Three Mile Island disaster in the United States and the Chernobyl disaster in the former Soviet Union now have high cancer rates. Russia has also now admitted that the former Soviet Union systematically dumped highly radioactive wastes into a river in Russia. No one knows how to clean this up, and scientists predict that eventually that waste will pollute the oceans of the world. So protection against radiation-induced cancer may become increasingly important in the coming century.

Antitumor Effects

Garlic extracts or its constituents also have direct antitumor effects, indicating that garlic may be useful for treatment as well as prevention of cancer. This, of course, only verifies what Hippocrates told us more than two thousand years ago. One common method of cancer research is to transplant tumors into a mouse, and then see if the garlic kills the tumors or impairs their growth. This test proves nothing about prevention, because the tumor has already formed. It is a good method for testing how practical a chemotherapeutic substance might be for humans, because toxicity and side effects can be observed in a real living system. This method is more reliable than test-tube experiments against single cancer cells, because it resembles more closely the actual conditions of cancer in the human body. Sometimes this research is done on strains of mice that are genetically susceptible to certain cancers, rather than implanting tumors.

One such animal study showed that garlic actually shrank the size of tumors. Dr Benjamin Lau, a professor at California's Loma Linda University School of Medicine, conducted a trial that applied physical stress to mice that had cancer. One group of mice received garlic in their diet for a week before the trial and also during the course of the thirty-five day trial. The tumors of both groups of mice continued to grow for the first two weeks. The tumors of the garlic-fed mice stabilized at that time, and after another week began to shrink. The tumors of the mice that did not receive garlic grew steadily throughout the trial.

Several trials showed that the survival time of tumor-implanted mice increased significantly with dietary garlic administration. In one of the trials, the researchers gave both oral and injectable garlic extracts to the mice; tumor growth decreased by 30 to 50 percent in the group that received injections and by 10 to 25 percent in those that received dietary garlic. This demonstrates that dietary amounts are clinically effective and that cancer patients might benefit by taking garlic along with other treatments their physician may prescribe.

ANTICANCER MECHANISMS

Scientists have not proven what the antitumor mechanisms in garlic are, but some theories have emerged. Our friend sulfur comes up again here. Some tumors are very high in sulfur compounds themselves, and scientists theorize that the sulfur compounds in garlic confuse the cancer cell and inactivate reproduction of the cell. Both allicin and ajoene in garlic may have this effect.

Another mechanism may be through the selenium content of garlic. Selenium alone exhibits a broad spectrum of anticancer effects even when administered in extremely small amounts—as low as one to five parts per million in the diet. A primary researcher on selenium, Dr. Clement Ip of the Department of Surgical Oncology, Roswell Park Cancer Institute, Buffalo, New York, has helped shift attention in recent years to the selenium in garlic. One reason is that selenium in foods may be superior to selenium in its inorganic form.

Dr. Ip found that organic selenium from garlic had a higher cancer-preventing potential than inorganic, elemental selenium. He used a selenium-enriched garlic developed at Cornell University in Ithaca, New York. It was grown on a selenium-enhanced fertilizer medium. He found that the selenium-enriched garlic inhibited mammary cancer in rats more than regular garlic did. This demonstrates that the selenium in garlic definitely can have an effect on tumors.

Very notably, the tissue levels of selenium were lower in the rats fed the garlic than in those fed selenite (the inorganic form), even though the anticancer effect was higher in the first group. This is good news for people who want to supplement selenium, because there is some concern with selenium toxicity in high doses and with long-term use. Selenium-enriched garlic may provide a higher effective dose with lower tissue accumulation and thus a lower toxic potential. Of course, garlic has many "side benefits" that inorganic selenium does not.

IMMUNE ENHANCEMENT

See "Garlic and the Immune System," Chapter 8, for how garlic helps the immune system fight off free-floating tumor cells seeking a new home.

GARLIC, CHEMOTHERAPY, AND RADIATION

One final thought on cancer is that garlic can help prevent some of the symptoms and side effects of chemotherapy treatments. These treatments often cause extreme discomfort. They are given to kill cancer cells, but they also attack many other cells in the body. In one study in Japan, garlic was given to a group of women who received chemotherapy and radiation therapy. Those patients who took the garlic had fewer side effects than those who did not. In fact, 67 percent of the women taking garlic reported no side effects at all.

CHAPTER 11

Stress, Fatigue, and Aging

We've seen in previous chapters that garlic has been used since ancient times as a tonic—a medicine to strengthen the system in general rather than to fight a particular disease. The slaves building the pyramids in ancient Egypt consumed garlic for this reason, and at one time threatened a strike against their masters when their garlic ration was reduced. Modern Ayurvedic and Unani practitioners still use garlic as a tonic, as we saw in Chapters 3 and 4.

A tonic is different from a *stimulant,* although both kinds of medicine appear to give energy. A stimulant, like the caffeine in coffee, tea, or soft drinks, gives quick energy that is followed by fatigue or depression. A tonic, on the other hand, builds energy slowly and steadily, over a matter of weeks or months, and it is not followed by a "crash." Tonics like garlic can act through many mechanisms, such as improving digestion, providing special nutrients for the body's fight against stress, or improving general resistance to disease.

Recent scientific trials have supported the idea that garlic is a tonic—that it can reduce the symptoms of stress, improve energy levels, reduce fatigue, improve athletic performance, and extend life expectancy.

STRESS

Stress is a natural part of life. When faced with a life-threatening situation, the body's *sympathetic* nervous system becomes predominant. This hastens the release of energy, increases blood flow to the muscles, and prepares the body for a short period of extreme exertion. This "fight or flight" response, if severe enough, enables a person under stress to perform superhuman acts, such as lifting a car off an injured person or heroically saving the lives of fellow soldiers. Less serious situations, such as an important crisis on the job, an impending deadline, or the urgent needs of children in the home, also involve this sympathetic response. Under ideal conditions of stress, such situations are rare, and when the danger has passed, the body can return to a more normal state. When resting, relaxing, eating, or sleeping, the *parasympathetic* system is predominant. During this phase, the body builds and repairs and stores up energy for future use.

Unfortunately, many of us remain locked in the sympathetic state as we meet the complexity of modern civilization. Our ancestors only faced life-threatening stress occasionally, during hunting or warfare, and spent much of their time relaxing. Anthropologists say that the hunter-gatherer predecessors worked a three-day week and spent the rest of the time in sport, recreation, music and dancing, family life, or ritual. Many of us today relax only rarely, working more than forty hours a week in high-stress jobs or family situations. We don't relax or enjoy exercise enough, or our relaxation is of poor quality, such as watching television. The result is exhaustion, indigestion, insomnia, depletion of the immune system, chronic illness, and other ill effects of a prolonged sympathetic state. The remedy, of course, is stress management and improved quality and quantity of rest and relaxation. Tonic herbs and foods are also appropriate for this condition and for any condition accompanied by depleted energy.

ANIMAL TRIALS

Scientific trials measuring the response of animals to stress have shown that garlic can reduce ill effects such as fatigue, loss of coordination, and appetite loss. I will not describe the trials in detail, because of the cruel nature of some of the stresses applied to the animals. I only pray that the information learned from these trials might benefit animals and humans in a greater measure than these animals suffered. The trials subjected mice to environmental, physical, and psychological stresses that normally produce fatigue, appetite loss, immune depression, weight loss, and loss of coordination. The mice treated with garlic extracts resisted fatigue during exercise tests and recovered from fatigue faster than mice on normal diets. They also better resisted stress from cold and cleared alcohol from their systems faster.

Reduced Stress on the Adrenal Glands

Dr. Benjamin Lau of the Loma Linda University Medical School in California has also experimented with the stress-reducing effects of garlic. One measure of stress is the output of the adrenal glands, the glands mainly responsible for our fight or flight response when we face life-threatening situations. The adrenal glands can flood our bloodstream with *adrenaline* and other substances that increase our metabolism and give strength. The blood level of these adrenal stress hormones is a good measure of the amount of stress an individual is undergoing.

Dr. Lau subjected two groups of mice to stress using a conventional stress-inducing machine. One group had been fed garlic for a week before the test. At the end of a week of stress (ten minutes per hour), the garlic-treated mice had blood levels of the stress hormones only one-fifth that of the regular mice. Thus, garlic was very potent in reducing the stress. It isn t clear whether the garlic actually directly affected the adrenal glands or whether it reduced stress through some other mechanism and the response required by the adrenals was indirectly lowered.

Stress and Fatigue

One of the first symptoms of stress is fatigue. The body cannot maintain a sympathetic state indefinitely, and this high-energy state eventually depletes the energy reserves. In the face of prolonged stress month after month and year after year, exhaustion is the natural result, and it is a sign that something must be changed in the life. A number of clinical trials have shown that garlic can reduce stress-related fatigue.

In one trial, the time mice could swim to exhaustion, both in a normal state and with stress to their hearts, was greatly improved. The mice who had eaten garlic juice or oil for a week could swim almost twice as long as normal mice;

and the garlic-treated mice with cardiac stress could swim seven times longer!

FATIGUE TRIALS IN HUMANS

Many antifatigue trials have also been conducted on humans, especially in Japan. In a trial in the early 1980s, more than a thousand patients who came to clinics at seven different university hospitals complaining of fatigue, depression, and anxiety received garlic extracts along with vitamins. At the end of a month, 50 to 80 percent of the patients reported a reduction in their symptoms. In 1982, researchers at Tokyo University medical school gave a garlic extract with vitamins for four weeks to eighteen patients who complained of fatigue and other psychosomatic complaints that interfered with daily life. In the overall judgment of effectiveness, nine of the patients said the garlic was effective, six said it was slightly effective, and only three said it was not effective.

The Many Symptoms of Stress

In a similar trial, in 1983, 122 patient with a variety of diagnoses were given garlic extract for four to eight weeks. The patients, who ranged in age from twenty to eighty-nine years, all had symptoms related to stress, fatigue, and general malaise—symptoms which conventional medicine has difficulty explaining and treating in many cases. Following is a list of the symptoms measured: general fatigue, eyestrain, shortness of breath, stiff shoulder, headache, low back pain, general debility, constipation, dizziness, appetite loss, numbness of limbs, cold limbs.

In the combined results, 85.2 percent of the patients reported better than "fair" improvement of their symptoms. The symptoms that responded best were fatigue (90.7 percent reported improvement), general physical discomfort (85.7 percent), cold feeling in the limbs (83.3 percent), and low back pain (82.5 percent). Among those who reported "markedly effective improvement," fatigue, general discomfort, and the tendency to constipation improved much more than the other symptoms. In the combined totals, systemic and neuromuscular complaints improved more than other symptoms. Some patients in this trial took garlic for only four weeks, and others took it for eight weeks. Those who took it for the longer time reported better results.

In a larger Japanese study with the same design as the one mentioned previously, and which included patients from some of the earlier studies, 1,050 patients with the various unexplained complaints were given garlic and vitamins for four to eight weeks. The same symptoms were examined as in the trial just mentioned. The results showed the steady improvement of the symptoms as the trial progressed. Improvement was judged to be remarkable, moderate, slight, none, or worse. The following table shows the improvement in symptoms over five weeks of the trial:

WEEK	IMPROVEMENT	IMPROVEMENT MORE THAN SLIGHT
1	41.2%	18.1%
2	58.3%	33.2%
4	67.1%	43.9%
5	71.4%	52.3%

The percentages in the "improvement more than slight" category mean that the patient's symptoms either went from "severe" to "slight" or from "moderate" to "no symptom." The chart shows that for more than half the patients, their symptoms either disappeared completely or became "slight." Researchers noted that those who took the garlic and vitamins for longer continued to improve. Of the individual symptoms, the greatest improvement was seen in "general fatigue" and "debility."

Exercise-Induced Fatigue

So far, we've only discussed fatigue due to unspecified stresses. Now let's look at a study where garlic reduced fatigue in athletes. The researchers took a group of twenty college athletes in Japan and divided them into two groups of ten. One group received garlic extract and the other took a placebo. The subjects then underwent identical vigorous exercise routines for two to three hours a day for three weeks. Researchers measured their level of fatigue afterwards using both a subjective questionnaire evaluation and objective medical and laboratory tests.

Both groups had less fatigue at the end of the training, reflecting the benefits of training. The garlic group, however, had significantly less fatigue than the placebo group. Such measures as tired body and weakness in the legs gradually decreased in the garlic group and then disappeared by the end of the test. The patellar reflex—in which the doctor hits below your knee with a small rubber hammer—improved steadily in the garlic group but decreased in the placebo group. (This reflex is a good measure of the general level of fatigue in the body.) Finally, garlic prevented the rise in liver enzymes and lactic acid that usually accompany fatigue.

Massive Stress

Garlic has also reduced the ill effects of massive stress. As I mentioned in Chapter 10, several trials have shown that garlic can reduce the ill effects of chemotherapy. This therapy puts tremendous stress on the organism, and the psychological stress on cancer patients at this stage of their disease is also severe. In one group of women receiving therapy for ovarian cancer, garlic prevented side effects completely for 67 percent of them. In another case, the debility and wasting that usually accompanies such treatment was reduced in a man with cancer of the head and neck. Researchers measured the levels of adrenal stress hormones in that patient and found that the garlic extract lowered their levels in the blood. This hormonal effect was similar to the one Dr. Lau found in his stress trial of mice discussed previously.

AGING AND FREE RADICALS

Besides the obvious that garlic can extend life by preventing serious illness, recent research suggests that garlic can thwart the aging process itself. A major contributor to aging is the process of destruction of cell membranes by free radicals.

Free radicals are highly charged molecules that set off destructive chain reactions in the fat molecules of cell membranes. They are produced by the normal body metabolism;

a diet high in cooked oils is also high in free radicals. As we age, the amount of free radicals in our bodies increases, and enzymes that counteract them also increase. Antioxidant vitamins like vitamins C, A, and E, and the mineral selenium all protect against free radical damage.

Garlic also contains potent free radical-destroying substances. One is the mineral selenium, and garlic has one of the highest selenium contents in common foods. Several other garlic constituents also have antioxidant properties in the test tube. I've listed a number of scientific references for garlic's antioxidant ability at the end of the book.

In an animal trial of aging in mice, garlic-treated mice lived longer than those with a normal diet. The researchers explored the idea that garlic's antioxidant effects might be involved, and sure enough, they found that both free radicals and antioxidant enzyme activity were lower in the garlic-treated mice, suggesting an antioxidant effect was in fact occurring. The test also indicated that garlic protected the mice against age-related memory loss.

The life-prolonging effects of garlic are not limited to laboratory animals. According to Dr. John Heinerman in *The Healing Benefits of Garlic*, the late sociologist Belle Boone Beard surveyed some 8,500 people who had lived to be more than one hundred years old. She requested information on their eating habits and found that the two foods that stood out were garlic and onions (*Science* 206:1057, November 30, 1979).

The research in this chapter shows that garlic is more than a simple medicine for specific diseases. Garlic is a tonic in the true sense of the word—it increases energy, well-being, and general health slowly but surely over weeks, months, and years.

CHAPTER 12

GARLIC CONSTITUENTS

Although people and physicians throughout the world have known for at least thirty-five centuries that you have to chop or crush garlic to release its medicinal properties, scientists only uncovered the main keys to its chemistry about fifty years ago. Chemical studies have verified that garlic is a "wonder plant" that outshines the so-called wonder drugs of the twentieth century; garlic contains more than thirty medicinally active compounds. Research so far has substantiated the medical uses of the Mesopotamians, Egyptians, and ancient Greeks, Romans, and Chinese. Scientists today have identified some of the biochemical pathways in which garlic helps our most serious modern diseases such as atherosclerosis, cancer, and chronic immune deficiencies.

THE SECRET OF GALEN'S WINE

Chemists first started picking garlic apart in 1844 when the German Theodor Wertheim extracted an oily substance from garlic cloves. He did this by boiling crushed garlic in water, collecting and cooling the steam, and then separating the volatile oils that had evaporated from the garlic along with the steam. The resulting oil had the strong smell of sulfur. He named the oil *allyl-sulfur*. The allyl part of the name came from *allium*, the latin name for garlic. That prefix has stuck, and today many of the dozens of compounds extracted from garlic, as well as similar nongarlic compounds, have "allyl" in their names. Wertheim had discovered an important fact about garlic: the key to its chemistry, to its odor, and to much of its medicinal action lies in its sulfur content.

In 1892, another German chemist, F. W. Semmler, discovered several more sulfur-containing compounds in garlic, but the greatest breakthroughs in research came in the 1940s. During that decade, pharmaceutical company researchers in the United States and Switzerland discovered the three substances aliin, allinase, and allicin. The interaction of these three compounds explains why the Roman physician Galen's garlic wine poultices (discussed in Chapter 1) saved the lives of many gladiators.

Aliin is the main sulfur-containing compound in raw garlic. It is odorless and makes up about one-fourth of one percent of the weight of garlic. Allinase is an enzyme whose purpose seems to be to break down aliin and other garlic compounds when garlic is crushed or cut. Allinase interacts with aliin in fresh-cut garlic to form allicin. Allicin is the compound that gives cut garlic its odor and its sharp, biting taste. Allicin is also a very potent medicinal agent, effective against bacteria, viruses, molds, yeasts, and other organisms.

The reason for this aliin-to-allicin transformation, from the plant's point of view, is self-defense. If a mold, plant virus, or bacterium attacks the bulb, the injury will cause the release of allicin, which will kill the invader. Likewise, if insects or animals go after the bulb, as soon as they break its skin, the released allicin will drive them away through its odor, taste, or toxic effects. Allicin is a potent insecticide.

The best way to extract allicin from garlic is to let chopped or crushed garlic sit in a mixture of water and alcohol for a few hours. This is exactly how Galen prepared garlic to dress the wounds of the gladiators—he placed crushed garlic in wine. Thus he released garlic's potent antibiotic effects and used them to fight infection 1,600 years before germs or antibiotics were discovered.

The Breakdown of Allicin

For decades, scientists thought of allicin as *the* active medicinal component of garlic, and much research was done into its antibiotic, antifungal, and anticancer effects. Newer discoveries have extended the list of garlic compounds to more than four hundred, with at least thirty of them having known medicinal properties. Most of garlic's medicinal constituents result from the breakdown of allicin.

Allicin itself is extremely important to the medicinal action of fresh garlic. It is highly unstable, however. Half of it degrades within three hours at room temperature, and it degrades almost completely within twenty-four hours. It also breaks down completely within twenty minutes at higher temperatures, such as in cooking. The degradation, however, produces new components—more than twenty of them are currently known—with a wide variety of medicinal effects. Allicin's breakdown turns garlic into an entire pharmacy of new medicinal constituents. This process also contributed to Galen's wine poultices and attests to the genius of the early herbalists, because they let the garlic soak in wine overnight.

The next day, the wine contained not only allicin, but many of its valuable by-products as well.

SULFUR COMPOUNDS

Allicin and its breakdown products all contain the element sulfur in a form that readily interacts with important enzyme systems in the human body. These sulfur-containing compounds are also responsible for garlic's odor, whether from cut garlic on your counter, the garlic on your breath after a garlic-rich meal, or the garlic in the sweat and on the breath of a regular garlic eater. We'll see more about garlic odor in Chapter 13, but know now that the odor is a sign that garlic's medicinal properties are at work throughout the body, protecting the body from cancer, heart disease, infection, and toxins. Garlic is one of the richest vegetable sources of sulfur. In Table 12.1, all the constituents with "allyl" in their names contain sulfur molecules.

Garlic's sulfur compounds contain structures typical of major enzymes and hormones that regulate body function, especially in the processes of detoxification and immune response. We discuss in Chapter 8 how some of these compounds stimulate the immune system. In Chapter 9, we see how garlic's constituents inhibit the production of cholesterol, thin the blood, and act as antioxidants. In Chapter 10, I describe some ways that these constituents help the body fight cancer. One common thread among the sulfur compounds is that they act upon *prostaglandins*, fatty acids in the body that regulate blood pressure, metabolism, temperature, fertility, and cell division. In conditions like cancer, asthma, and blood clot formation, prostaglandin activity becomes rampant. Garlic compounds interfere with this out-of-control process.

TABLE 12.1

KNOWN ACTIVE CONSTITUENTS OF GARLIC AND THEIR ACTIONS. ALL CONSTITUENTS ARE NOT PRESENT IN ALL FORMS OF GARLIC.

	Antibiotic	Detoxifies	Inhibits cancer	Antioxidant	Lowers blood sugar	Lowers cholesterol	Thins blood	Protects the liver
ajoene	x	x	x			x	x	
allicin	x	x	x		x	x	x	
aliin		x		x				
allixin		x	x					
allyl mercaptan		x	x					
allyl methyl thiosulfinate	x							
allyl methyl trisulfide		x	x					
allyl propyl disulfide					x			
diallyl disulfide		x	x			x		
diallyl hepta sulfide				x				
diallyl hexa sulfide				x				
diallyl penta sulfide				x				
diallyl sulfide			x					
diallyl tetra sulfide				x				
diallyl tri sulfide	x		x	x				x
dimethyl disulfide		x						

	Anti-biotic	Detox-ifies	Inhibits cancer	Anti-oxidant	Lowers blood sugar	Lowers choles-terol	Thins blood	Protects the liver
dimethyl trisulfide		x						
dipropyl disulfide		x						
methyl ajoene		x						
methyl allyl thiosulfinate	x							
propyline sulfide			x					
2-vinyl-4H-1,3,-dithiin							x	
3-vinyl-4H-1,2-dithiin							x	
S-allyl cysteine		x	x	x		x		
S-allyl cysteine sulfoxide					x			
S-allyl mercapto								
cysteine				x				

A Table of Constituents

As you can see in Table 12.1, most of the constituents have two or more overlapping functions. Allicin has the widest activity in the table, but this may simply be because it has been studied more than the other compounds. *Ajoene* is another much-studied constituent, with a wide variety of actions. Scientists identified ajoene in garlic in the mid-1980s. They used high heat and chemical solvents to obtain it, and some popular writers have said that it does not exist in normal garlic preparations. However, researchers have recently identified ajoene in certain commercial garlic oil products and fresh preparations. Constituents may very well have more actions than are listed, but they have not been tested for them. Some major constituents of garlic have not yet been identified. Remember that not all the compounds in the table are present in all forms of garlic. In Chapters 14 and 15, I describe some of the different forms and suggest which ones are most appropriate for different conditions.

ALL THE FACTS ARE NOT IN

Scientists today know that some of garlic's most important medicinal effects are due to compounds that have not yet been identified. For example, in a paper presented at the Fourth Annual Phytotherapy Conference in Munich, Germany, in 1993, scientists described how some of garlic's ability to lower cholesterol and relax the smooth muscle in the arterial wall is not caused by these compounds. They only know that water-soluble compounds are responsible. So the whole story has not been told of garlic's chemistry, and in another ten years we will have tested and found medicinal activity in many more constituents.

The bottom line on garlic constituents: The whole is greater than any of the parts. The constituents work together and have overlapping functions.

CHAPTER 13

Side Effects and Contraindications

Authors quote many other diseases garlic is good for, but conceal its vices.

Nicholas Culpepper, 1655 A.D.

Toxicity and side effects to herbal medicine is one of my professional specialties, and I have written and lectured widely on this topic both to physicians and to the general public. I classify three types of adverse reactions to herbs: *toxicity, side effects,* and *incompatibility.*

Toxicity

Toxicity, a reaction leading to serious illness or death, is extremely rare from medicinal herbs, and it is unknown with garlic. Herbs are certainly less toxic than conventional drugs; adverse reactions to prescribed drugs are responsible for about 8 percent of all hospital admissions—about two million patients a year. They kill as many as 100,000 people a year. Even over-the-counter medications kill or cause serious injury in tens of thousands of people annually. By comparison, any report of fatality due to an herbal medicine is extremely rare, certainly less than one case a year. A national poison control center computer database does not even have a category for adverse reactions to medicinal plants. The *AMA Handbook of Poisonous and Injurious Plants*, published by the American Medical Association, mentions only a handful of medicinal plants, and the most common reason is minor, possible skin irritation in sensitive individuals. As we'll see, garlic has no potential for toxicity unless it is taken in very large quantities—more than a bulb a day—for a long time. Garlic is classified by the United States Food and Drug Administration as *GRAS*: generally regarded as safe (for food use).

Overdoing It

The only real danger of serious systemic toxicity from garlic would come with long-term consumption of several bulbs or more of raw garlic a day, or the equivalent amount of juice. Several animal trials have shown that large doses of raw garlic or garlic juice can cause irritation to the stomach lining, poor assimilation of food, disruption of the healthy bacteria in the bowel, liver dysfunction, and anemia. These were artificial experiments with force-feeding of the animals. The problem is naturally self-limiting in humans, the discomfort will make you stop taking garlic before it causes serious harm. However, earlier in this century in the United States, physicians experimented with raw garlic juice as a treatment for tuberculosis. After taking a high dose of the juice continuously, the equivalent of several bulbs of garlic a day, the patients became anemic. Some patients in clinical trials have taken the equivalent of two bulbs of garlic a day, in the form of juice, without ill effects, but this was only for a short time (a month or less). The main problem, then, is to think that if a little is good, then a lot is better, taking heroic doses of raw garlic for a long time.

SIDE EFFECTS

Any herb strong enough to act as a medicine is strong enough to produce side effects. Because garlic is such a potent medicine, you can be sure that it can cause side effects. The most common are stomach irritation, nausea, garlic odor on the breath, skin irritation, and possibly even skin burns. Anyone will experience these who takes garlic in a high enough dose or for a long enough time. The following describes the side effects and contraindications for garlic.

Side Effects of Garlic

Almost anyone will experience the following side effects to garlic with a high enough dose and a long enough application:

- diarrhea
- flatulence
- flushed face
- gastric irritation
- headache
- heartburn
- hot skin
- increased sexual desire
- insomnia

- nausea
- rapid pulse
- skin blisters (external applications)
- skin irritation (external applications)
- vomiting

Garlic Burns

The most serious side effect from normal use of garlic is burns on the skin. This is common among kitchen workers who cut large quantities of garlic, especially in Asian restaurants. Serious burns can also occur when using garlic as a home remedy, and even herbalists are not immune from using it improperly. I know of a woman who heard that a garlic poultice on the chest was good for a chest cold. She applied crushed garlic directly to her ten-month-old baby's chest. Eventually the baby started screaming, and a layer of skin was blistered off her chest.

I also know of a British herbalist who applied a garlic poultice to a wart and left it overnight. The next day, the herbalist had third-degree burns, complete destruction of the healthy tissue around the wart, but had felt no discomfort under the bandage. As we see in Chapter 14, garlic poultices should be applied only with caution and not for longer than twenty minutes. One report in the scientific literature tells of eight cases of patients in Hong Kong who developed inflammation after rubbing the cut end of a fresh garlic bulb onto the skin to treat fungal and other infections of the groin, neck, lower limb, hand, or face. Their irritation was not as severe as the cases mentioned above, but they were nevertheless severe enough to seek medical assistance for the burn.

CONTRAINDICATIONS

Certain symptoms or illnesses indicate that you should not use garlic as a medicine. See "Contraindications for Garlic" for a list of these.

Large quantities of garlic or long-term use of medicinal quantities is not recommended in people with the following conditions:

- acute inflammation
- brittle diabetes
- dehydration
- hypoglycemia
- impending surgery
- insomnia
- organ transplant
- pemphigus
- use of blood-thinning drugs

Inflammation

Writers throughout history have cautioned against using garlic during acute inflammation and pain. I once had a patient who had suffered from rheumatoid arthritis for twenty years. She had flushed cheeks, warm hands and feet, and a "fiery" disposition. She had successfully managed her periodic outbreaks of arthritis with diet, short-term vegetable fasts, and hydrotherapy (walking in the cool water of a swimming pool). Before she came to me, she had read that garlic was "good for you," and that it was even "good for arthritis." Garlic is traditionally used for arthritis, but not internally—something she did not know. Garlic plasters and poultices can be used as a counterirritant on the skin over the painful part. This draws circulation to the area and may soothe the pain. Instead, she took garlic powder capsules for about a week. Her arthritis pain became so acute that she considered getting a prescription painkiller, which she had not had to use in more than ten years. When she stopped the garlic, however, the pain decreased within a day and was at tolerable levels again soon after that.

Hypoglycemia, Brittle Diabetes

Garlic lowers blood sugar and may be a helpful addition to other therapies for most cases of diabetes. It should be used in medicinal amounts only under medical supervision in brittle diabetes, which has characteristic swings from high to low blood sugar. A large dose of garlic could lower the blood sugar at the wrong time in the cycle, promoting hypoglycemic shock. I'll talk more about this under "Diabetes" in Chapter 15.

Hypoglycemia means abnormally low blood sugar. It may be a primary condition, or it may accompany another disease. People with low blood sugar may exhibit nervous symptoms, such as light-headedness and palpitations or sometimes mental confusion and inappropriate behavior. If you have a medical diagnosis of hypoglycemia, use medicinal amounts of garlic, especially large amounts of raw garlic, only after discussing it with your doctor.

Pemphigus

Pemphigus is a relatively rare autoimmune disorder in which the immune system causes lesions in the skin and mucous membranes. Doctors know that drugs with active *thiol group*—the same sulfur formation that gives garlic constituents much of their activity—is capable of inducing an attack of pemphigus. Patients with this condition might also avoid onions, leeks, and other related plants.

Blood-Thinning Medications

As we see in Chapter 9, garlic is a potent blood thinner, even in dietary amounts. People taking blood-thinning drugs, such as might be prescribed after a stroke, heart attack, or episode of blood clots, should consult with their physician before taking large amounts of garlic. Garlic could effectively make such a medication more potent and cause side effects. Adverse effects of blood-thinning medications are among the most common causes of admission to a hospital for drug side effects.

Impending Surgery

If you have a scheduled elective surgery coming up, it might be wise to stop taking garlic for a week beforehand. Garlic is a blood thinner and slows blood clotting time. Clotting of the blood is extremely important in surgery to prevent bleeding complications either during the surgery or afterwards.

Organ Transplants

After an organ transplant, the body's immune system naturally attacks the transplanted tissue. Standard medical therapy is to suppress the patient's immune system after the transplant. The body's natural killer cells are mainly responsible for the rejection mechanism, and we see in Chapter 8 that large amounts of garlic dramatically increase the activity of these cells. Transplant patients shouldn't take garlic, especially in medicinal amounts, without medical supervision.

CAUTIONS ON GARLIC

What some famous physicians have said about garlic:

Hippocrates, 400 B.C.

The "Father of Western Medicine" warned that garlic "arouses wind, causes heat in the chest and heaviness in the head, can aggravate and increase existing pain, and also increases the urine."

Dioscorides, 50 A.D.

The author of the most famous Roman herbal warned that garlic can injure the stomach through "dryness" and cause excessive thirst.

Pliny, 50 A.D.

This great Roman naturalist cautioned that garlic can dull the eyesight, cause gas, injure the stomach, and cause excessive thirst.

Galen, 200 A.D.

The most famous of the Roman physicians warned of the possible irritating and drying side effects of garlic and recommended that it be cooked or boiled briefly until it loses its sharp qualities.

Ibn Sina (Avicenna), 1000 A.D.

This Persian master physician considered garlic to be heating and drying and said that raw garlic was too strong for most people's systems. He recommended garlic cooked or in milk.

John Gerard, 1600 A.D.

Gerard wrote the most famous of the English language herbals. He cautioned that garlic can be overly heating for some individuals. He says it "engendereth naughty and sharp blood for such as are of that complexion."

Nicholas Culpepper, 1650 A.D.

Culpepper warned against excessive use of garlic, saying that in people with hot and dry constitutions it will cause great aggravation. He especially warned against its drying properties. "Let it be taken internally with great moderation," he wrote.

William Cook, M.D., 1869 A.D.

Like professional physicians before his time, Cook cautioned that garlic can lead to overstimulation, flushed face, and headache. He said it should not be used internally during the existence of inflammation or acute irritation and should never be used for a long time.

INCOMPATIBILITY: MY STORY

Another category of possible adverse effects to herbs is incompatibility between the person and the herb. I'll tell my own story to illustrate this.

I once experimented with garlic to see how high a dose I could tolerate. I have a very hot constitution and have to approach garlic with caution. When other people need two blankets to stay warm at night, I kick off the sheets. On a cool fall day when others are getting out their jackets, I'm still in a T-shirt. I'm also in my late forties, and my blood cholesterol and triglycerides are getting higher each year in spite of regular exercise and a healthy diet. The men in my family are at a high risk for heart problems. I decided to treat myself with garlic for the high cholesterol, and started by adding a clove of garlic cooked in my meals most days and occasionally took a half or a whole clove raw, chopped, and added to a cup of soup or rice just before eating. Some days, I'd take up to five cloves cooked and raw.

I began to feel the tonic effects of the garlic (see Chapter 11) in a few days and felt some of my slight mucous congestion clear up. This felt very good to me, so I persisted.

However, some symptoms began to appear. At first I didn't attribute them to the garlic, even though I was performing a conscious experiment and looking for them. The first thing I noticed was some mental restlessness, which interfered with my stillness during prayer or meditation. My slight tendency to insomnia became a little worse. This persisted for a few weeks, and I became somewhat used to it.

Then one day I noticed blood on my toilet paper. This caused me a big scare because a person close to me and close to my age had recently been diagnosed with colon cancer. I went for a checkup, feeling nervous and insecure about my condition for the five days until the appointment. On examination, the doctor, a naturopathic physician, told me that for some reason, the mucous glands just above the rectum were very dry and that the high fiber in my diet was probably irritating the unlubricated tissue there. He suggested cutting down on fiber. However, I recognized that the reason for the drying up of the mucous there was the drying properties of the garlic, and I knew what to do. I cut down on the garlic. By now I liked it a lot, however, so I didn't cut it out completely.

A few weeks later (after herbal suppositories had helped heal my dehydrated rectal wall), I took larger doses again for a few days. Around this time I had mildly injured my shoulder and ribs while playing sports and I had a slight nerve inflammation between my ribs called intercostal neuritis. After a few days on a higher dose of garlic (five cloves cooked in food throughout the day), the neuritis became severe. It impaired my ability to sleep, to type, or to lift things with my left hand. I was in constant pain. I realized again what the problem was, the heat from the garlic was aggravating the inflammation. I went to my acupuncturist, who performed a procedure called *cupping* on my back to draw the heat and stagnation out of the inflamed area, and he also gave me acupuncture. I stopped eating garlic completely, and the condition was all but gone in two days. Then I continued acupuncture treatments for another week to disperse the restlessness and insomnia that had been bothering me ever since I started the garlic. I now can tolerate a half clove to a clove of garlic, but I continue to periodically take breaks from it completely.

TRADITIONAL SYSTEMS

My story has a number of lessons, and it is a good introduction to the incompatibilities of garlic. The most important is that most of my symptoms would never be listed as side effects. Someone grounded in a Western medical system, including most Western herbalists, would never associate rectal bleeding or intercostal neuritis with the garlic. *Anyone* trained in a traditional system, however, like Chinese, Ayurvedic, or Unani medicine, would recognize those immediately as signs of heat in the corresponding terminology of their system, give treatments to clear the heat, and recommend a more cooling and moistening diet. (See Chapters 2, 3, and 4 for more about these traditional systems.) A person with a cold or phlegmatic constitution would probably have never had these problems, and the higher dose of garlic would have been just fine for them. Below, I'll describe the type of person who is incompatible with garlic. If you've ever been in an incompatible marriage, or know someone who has, then you'll realize the potential for discomfort here.

Chinese "Deficient Yin"

Traditional Chinese practitioners say that garlic is contraindicated for patients who have a syndrome they call "deficient yin." People with this condition will feel weak and "burned out." They may have an emaciated appearance, dizziness, spots before the eyes, and a thin pulse like a thread. They also have signs of heat, are thirsty and dehydrated, have night sweats, insomnia and restlessness, hot hands and feet, flushed face, and a fast pulse. These symptoms may accompany many particular diseases, and when many of these symptoms appear as a pattern, garlic will make them worse. Other people with heat signs, such as hot hands and feet, flushed face, fast pulse, aversion to heat, and craving for cool food and drinks, may also tolerate garlic poorly. For more about Chinese medicine, see Chapter 2.

Ayurveda and the Pitta Type

I discussed Ayurveda, the traditional medicine of India, in Chapter 3. In this system of medicine, garlic is contraindicated in the pitta type of individual, especially when they have a pitta imbalance. Pitta in Ayurveda is similar to heat in Chinese medicine but not quite identical to it. Pitta individuals may have a red complexion, gums that bleed easily, dark yellow urine, diarrhea with a burning sensation, an argumentive disposition, anger, inflammatory diseases, and a strong pulse that feels like a taut wire. They should normally eat cooling and moistening foods and avoid hot spices such as garlic.

The Four Humors

The four humors system of the Greeks, Arabs, and Persians classifies patients in four general categories (we talk more about this in Chapter 4). The *phlegmatic* constitution is cold and moist, the *sanguine* constitution is hot and moist, the *choleric* constitution is hot and dry, and the *melancholic* constitution is cold and dry. Garlic is contraindicated in the last two, hot-dry and cold-dry, because of its drying properties. The best way to diagnose these without training in the system is simply to watch for signs of dryness: dry mouth, thirst, dry mucous membranes, scanty urine, and so on. For an illustration, see the story in Chapter 4 about a woman with a mental disturbance that was made worse by garlic in her diet.

GARLIC AND SPIRITUAL PURSUITS

Although garlic has a worldwide reputation for keeping vampires and predatory spirits away, it is forbidden in some esoteric spiritual traditions, especially those of the monastic type. One saying in Tibet is that garlic should not be brought into a monastery even if the person carrying it were saving the building from burning. Garlic is also discouraged among Zen practitioners in Japan and among Hindu monks. The priestly class in the Hindu religion and monks in the Jain religions also avoid it.

The reason for this is twofold. First, these monks sit for hours in meditation each day performing inner exercises to detach from the world. Garlic is very grounding mentally and stimulating physically, and it makes it harder for the monks to detach and sit still. Second, monks and nuns in these traditions are usually celibate. Because garlic is heating and sexually stimulating, it is overly irritating for them.

If you are pursuing meditation or if you are single and celibate, you might try eliminating garlic and onions along with heavy meat from your diet and see if it doesn't make life easier for you.

WHAT TO DO IF YOU'RE GARLIC-INTOLERANT

If you don't tolerate garlic well, but you want to take advantage of its medicinal benefits, don't give up hope. Here are some things to try:

- Take only a small amount. A half-clove of garlic a day confers most of the long-term health benefits. If you're taking a commercial preparation and it doesn't agree with you, take a smaller dose.
- Take your raw garlic in milk, carrot juice, or honey. These cut down on irritating gastric symptoms.
- Take garlic water. Start with one clove, chopped up and put into hot water at bedtime. Let it sit overnight. Then drink the water (but not the chopped clove). Work up to two to four cloves in the water.
- Take garlic wine or vinegar. See Chapter 14 for how to prepare this.
- Try cooked instead of raw garlic. In one clinical trial, researchers found that garlic retained most of its blood-thinning properties even after cooking.
- For a cold or flu, take a garlic steam, inhalation, foot bath, foot poultice, chest plaster, or garlic vinegar on the skin. You'll find directions for these in Chapter 14.
- Take your garlic only part of the time. Most people find garlic too heating after taking it for a while. Take regular breaks. Take garlic for three days at a time. Take it only

when someone in your house or office has a cold or flu. This will give some tonic effect, but it will not treat serious conditions like atherosclerosis.

• Try Kyolic garlic. This is an aged garlic extract from Japan that has most of the heating principles removed. Kyolic does not contain many of the beneficial constituents of garlic, but dozens of clinical trials have proven its general benefit. It is not as effective for antibiotic purposes as other forms. Its tonic properties are well established, however, and it is less irritating than other forms. The following statistics, from two clinical trials in Japan, show the very low rate of side effects for Kyolic, even after several months of daily use.

SIDE EFFECTS TO KYOLIC GARLIC

TRIAL #1: 130 PATIENTS (FOUR WEEKS)*

	Marked	Moderate	Slight	Total
Gastric discomfort	1	2	9	12
Diarrhea, soft feces	1		2	3
Nausea		1	1	2
Insomnia			1	1
Hot feeling	1			1

*Only six patients dropped out of the study due to side effects.

TRIAL #2: 1,050 PATIENTS (FOUR TO EIGHT WEEKS)*

Gastrointestinal upset	72 cases	7.0%
Nausea	28 cases	2.7%
Diarrhea	14 cases	1.4 %
Belching	6 cases	0.6%

*Twenty-five cases (2.5%) dropped out of the trial because of the side effects.

GARLIC BREATH

In the French court of King Louis XIV (the "Sun King") the royal chef had an unusual practice. After preparing a salad for the King, he would chew up a clove of garlic and then breathe over the salad. This would give the flavor of garlic to the salad without subjecting the king to the embarrassment of garlic on his breath.

This story demonstrates the worldwide social stigma against garlic breath—a taboo that is not limited to European countries. In the Islamic world, it is considered poor etiquette to attend congregational prayers with the strong smell of garlic on the breath. In China, the southern Chinese look down on the "garlic-eating" northern Chinese. Yet healers in all these cultures recognize garlic as a profound tonic medicine. The French chef was getting the full protective benefits of garlic against the ill effects of all the rich sauces he undoubtedly made and ate day after day. Garlic is a staple in the diet in Unani Tibb medicine of the Muslims. Albert L. Leung, author of *Chinese Herbal Remedies*, says that although as a child he would joke that you could detect a "northerner" miles away by the garlic smell, he and friends also envied the northerner's ability to resist colds.

Causes

The odor of garlic comes in two ways. When you first eat it, especially raw garlic, the odor remains in the mouth. Some odor also rises from the stomach with belching. After some time, however, the garlic constituents pass into the blood stream and penetrate literally to every cell in the body. At this stage, some of them are excreted through the lungs and others through the sweat glands. This is responsible for the pervasive garlic odor of a regular garlic eater.

Remember that these substances are antibiotic, immune-stimulating, and protective to the circulatory system. This general garlic odor is a sign that the lungs and bronchial tract are being protected against infection, liver cells are protected from toxic damage, atherosclerosis is being retarded, and every cell in the body is being protected from cancer.

Here are some options for dealing with garlic breath:

• Get used to it. This is my first recommendation. Let your spouse and your whole family take it regularly, and enjoy your improved health together.

• Take it cooked instead of raw. This greatly reduces the odor.

• Cover it up. Try a commercial mouthwash if you like. Chewing parsley with garlic is a traditional cover-up. Rue, roasted coffee beans, parsley seeds, or cardamom seeds may also be effective.

• Take it in capsules. This will eliminate the mouth odor. Garlic powder capsules will have more odor than garlic oil capsules, but they'll also have more medicinal benefit.

• Take Kyolic garlic. This product does not have many of the sulfurous constituents that give garlic its odor. This form retains some of the circulatory, anticancer, and tonic effects of garlic, but it does not maintain the antibiotic activity.

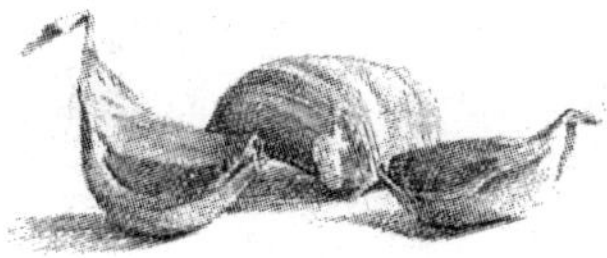

Garlic and Disease

In this section, I'll discuss the medicinal forms of garlic, including commercial products and tell you how to use them to treat your own minor health conditions. I'll also tell how they are used for more serious diseases, so you can work with your doctor in a more informed way if you have one of those conditions.

CHAPTER 14

The Many Forms of Garlic

In this chapter, I'll tell you how to make and use thirty-two different garlic forms at home. We'll see that the most effective products for acute illnesses, such as colds, flu, infections, or asthma, are raw garlic and do-it-yourself forms like garlic soaked overnight in wine or garlic tea. I'll also explain the various commercial garlic products available in stores. If you are garlic-sensitive (see Chapter 13 on side effects) and need to take garlic long-term, some of these products might be right for you. First, I'll discuss some of the issues that affect which form is best for you or your condition.

Antibiotic Properties

If you want to treat a cold, flu, bronchitis, vaginal infection, dysentery, ulcer, or other infectious disease, the garlic form you use should have antibiotic properties. Not all forms do.

As we saw in Chapter 12, the most important antibiotic constituent in garlic is allicin. Allicin is produced as soon as garlic is cut or chopped, but it normally degrades quickly into a large number of sulfur-containing by-products. These have medicinal properties, but most are not antibiotic. Some garlic powder products retain their allicin and theoretically could have antibiotic effects, but none can compare to the power, simplicity, and economy of making and taking your own raw garlic products. Garlic oils and aged garlic products do not contain allicin. One kind of garlic oil (macerated oil) is made by soaking chopped garlic in another oil such as soybean oil. This form contains a significant amount of ajoene, which may have antibiotic properties, but the amounts in the oils are so low that you might need to take a whole bottle at a time.

IRRITATION

Garlic can be severely irritating to some people. Sensitive individuals can even blister their skin with it. Individuals with hot and dry constitutions do not tolerate garlic well, especially long-term. So an important issue is whether the form of garlic you take is irritating for you. You may start to take garlic to bring down high cholesterol, only to find that you can't take it for more than a few days. In such a case, you may more easily tolerate a product that contains no allicin. See Table 14.1 for some examples. The mildest form of garlic is Kyolic garlic, an aged product from Japan. Allicin-free Kyolic products retain some cholesterol-lowering, anticancer, detoxifying, and tonic properties, but they have generally weaker medicinal effects than forms with some allicin and their by-products in them.

TABLE 14.1
GARLIC FORMS AND THEIR CONSTITUENTS

Forms	Constituents and Their Properties			
	Allicin and related compounds	Sulfides and related compounds	Ajoenes Dithiins	Other
All forms have some amount of immune-stimulating, anticancer, detoxifying, cholesterol-lowering, and blood-thinning properties				
	antibiotic blood-thinning blood-sugar-lowering	antioxidant blood-sugar lowering	antibiotic powerful blood-thinning	antioxidant
Fresh chopped garlic	X			X
Cooked garlic		X		X
Fresh garlic juice	X			X
Garlic juice (aged 3–24 hours)	X	X		X
Garlic juice (aged more than two days)		X		X
Infusion	X	X		X
Decoction		X		X

Forms	Constituents and Their Properties			
	Allicin and related compounds	Sulfides and related compounds	Ajoenes Dithiins	Other
Garlic wine (aged 3–18 hours)	X	X		X
Garlic wine (aged long-term) or tincture		X		X
Fresh garlic vinegar	X	X		X
Fresh macerated garlic oil (aged 3–36 hours)	X	X	X	X
Macerated garlic oil (some commercial brands)		small amounts	X	X
Steam-distilled garlic oil (most commercial brands)		X		X
Garlic powder	X	small amounts		X
Kyolic				X

Medicinal Strength

Every form of garlic tested has cardiovascular benefits and anticancer properties. This includes fresh, cooked, oil, major commercial brands, and even ordinary dried garlic powder. Garlic has a wide effective dose range, so dose is not normally a problem. With some commercial garlic powder and oil products, however, the amounts of medicinal constituents can vary widely. In one assay of products from the United States, one powder product contained only one-fourth of the allicin in another product. Garlic oils differed in constituents by a factor of more than twenty—you'd need to take twenty capsules of the one product to get the same dose as the other! I don't think of these variations as arguments to buy one brand or another, rather to use fresh or homemade products as much as possible. If you want a commercial product, however, you might select a name brand, such as Garlicin, Kwai, or Kyolic. These have all been tested in clinical trials or other studies and have therapeutic levels of active ingredients. The commercial products with the least strength are cheap powders and oils. Note that garlic cloves themselves have varying amounts of active constituents, depending on where and how they're grown, so even with cloves, you can have some variation in strength.

Commercial Products

A huge amount of misinformation about garlic products has been spread by competitors in the marketing war for the very lucrative garlic market in the United States. I'll try to clear up some of the resulting misconceptions later. First, let's look at the many commercial forms available.

Capsules Control Mouth Odor

All encapsulated garlic powders reduce the odor of garlic to some extent. The odor comes from three possible sources: bits of garlic left in the mouth after eating, garlic belched up from the stomach, and garlic excreted through the skin and on the breath. Swallowing powder in capsules automatically solves the problem of garlic in the mouth, probably the most offensive smell. Some capsules are also enteric-coated, meaning they have a coat that prevents them from being digested in the stomach. They only dissolve further down in the intestines, which prevents a garlic aftertaste and odor from the stomach. Effective products will not prevent garlic odor from the skin or lungs, however. If this odor is missing, so are many of the benefits of garlic. Either you're not taking enough, or the product is not delivering an effective form of garlic.

Allicin in Powdered Tablets

The aliin in cut, chopped, or ground garlic is very unstable at room temperature in the presence of moisture. It reacts with allinase to form allicin. The allicin is also unstable and breaks down within a day or two. Thus, companies have devised ways to preserve these valuable constituents in powdered garlic.

Dried Garlic One method is to neutralize the allinase after crushing the garlic. The aliin-containing mash can then be powdered and dried. Afterwards, allinase is added back in, but it will not react to form allicin until the capsule reaches the moisture of the digestive tract. Allicin is then formed directly in the intestines. No one knows with this form just how much allicin is actually released in the intestine, but it is not enough to achieve intestinal antibiotic effects.

Powder from Sliced Garlic With this method, the garlic is sliced instead of crushed. The allicin is formed and breaks down along the surface of the slice but not in the interior of the thin wafer. The slices are then dried at a cool temperature, and finally powdered and encapsulated. The thin slices make the drying process very efficient, so the aliin remains stable until the powder gets to the intestines. This form can be standardized for allicin-releasing potential, but like the form above, no one knows exactly how much allicin is actually formed in the intestine, and the amount is insufficient for antibiotic effects.

Stabilized Allicin Another method is to crush the garlic and allow the allicin to form. The allicin-rich powder is dried, and the allicin is stabilized in a proprietary process. The allicin is released in the digestive tract without having to undergo the reaction with allinase. This form can be standardized for its actual allicin content, yet these products do not work well clinically as antibiotics.

Oils

Two kinds of garlic oil are available in capsules or "pearls" in the United States. Oils contain none of the allicin, but they are rich in sulfur-containing breakdown products, which have many medicinal properties of their own.

Steam-Distilled Oils These are made by driving steam through a large quantity of crushed garlic. The heat of the steam causes all the allicin in the garlic to decompose into its sulfur-containing by-products. These are very volatile and are carried off by the steam. Later, they are separated from the condensed steam, mixed with a vegetable oil, and put into capsules. This kind of oil contains no allicin and has no direct antibiotic effects, although it will still increase the body's resistance to infection and disease.

Macerated Oils These are produced by soaking crushed or sliced garlic in a vegetable oil such as soybean oil. As with the other oils, the allicin breaks down, but in this case, instead of forming the strong-smelling sulfides of garlic oil, it forms classes of compounds called ajoenes and dithiins. Ajoenes have many of the properties of allicin, including some antibiotic properties. The ajoenes and dithiins are also the strongest known blood-thinning constituents in garlic. These are the weakest of the commercial garlic preparations, but they may be the best for patients who have had strokes or heart attacks who want to thin their blood. Because of the potent blood-thinning properties of ajoene, which is not present in significant amounts in raw garlic or in the other preparations, caution should be used if you are taking blood-thinning drugs.

Kyolic

Kyolic garlic, a deodorized form of garlic from Japan, contains no allicin, sulfides, ajoenes, or dithiins, but it retains other constituents. This can be both a plus and a minus. It means that Kyolic is probably not effective for antibiotic purposes in intestinal and other infections. However, Kyolic is less irritating for long-term use, such as cholesterol lowering and cancer prevention. Dozens of clinical trials and research studies have shown Kyolic to be effective as a tonic, cholesterol-lowering, and anticancer agent. For instance, Florida physician Dr. Tariq Abdullah gave healthy volunteers six Kyolic capsules a day, and then tested their blood for immune system activity. The natural killer cells in their blood, a key component of the immune system, killed more than twice the number of cancer cells in a lab dish as did the cells of volunteers who didn't take the garlic. I still recommend raw, cooked, or homemade garlic products, but Kyolic might be the best form for you if you don't tolerate garlic well but need to take it for a specific purpose like lowering cholesterol.

DEBUNKING THE "GARLIC WARS" PROPAGANDA

Companies selling garlic products have spent huge amounts of advertising dollars in their war for a share of the $100 million annual garlic market in the United States. Their efforts also have included sponsoring scientific trials and then using the results to claim superiority over other products. Much pseudoscientific information has made its way into magazine articles and books about garlic. Remember, every form of garlic tested, with or without a particular constituent, including garlic fried in your frying pan, has cardiovascular benefits and anticancer properties. Here are some claims and the truth behind them.

"Our Garlic is Odorless"

The odor in garlic comes first from food residues in the mouth, then from garlic in the stomach, and finally from sulfur constituents excreted through the skin and lungs. All capsules, if swallowed, eliminate the mouth odor. Those that are enteric-coated eliminate the odor from the stomach. All products containing allicin or its sulfur by-products (see Table 14.1) will produce odor from the lungs and the skin if you take them in medicinal quantities.

"Allicin is Unstable"

Some companies dispute other companies' claims to have allicin in their product, saying that allicin is too unstable for capsules. Allicin is very unstable with any heat or at room temperature in the presence of moisture. Some products have the allicin dried and stabilized, however. Most have some kind of "allicin potential," meaning that they contain alliin and allinase in stable dried powder, and these will form allicin in the digestive tract. It is true that the amounts of allicin actually released in the intestine are unpredictable, but it is present in some amount in the product categories that claim to have it.

"Their Product Has No Allicin or Sulfides"

One company successfully demonstrated that another company's product contained no allicin or any of its breakdown products. The implication is that the second company's product is worthless, when in fact that product has been proven effective for a number of conditions in clinical trials and other studies.

"Allicin is Toxic"

A company that makes an allicin-free product has circulated statements that allicin is toxic. This may be true of isolated allicin in a test tube or of allicin-rich garlic force-fed through tubes into the stomach of mice, but the allicin in commercial products has no toxic potential. In some parts of the world, people regularly eat a bulb or more of garlic a day without ill effect. Allicin can be irritating to some people, and for them an allicin-free product might be helpful.

A Bottom Line

Dr. Subhuti Dharmananda, director of the Immune Enhancement Project in Portland, Oregon, regularly treats AIDS patients with opportunistic infections. The main antibiotic therapy he uses is garlic, and he finds it very effective to prevent or treat these infections. He started out trying to use an encapsulated form of garlic standardized for its allicin content, one of the better products. He found, however, that even doses of twenty-seven capsules a day had no effect on the infections. When he switched to raw garlic at the same dose, he got the desired result. The bottom line is this: if you want antibiotic effects, use raw garlic or one of the homemade forms. If you want blood-thinning or cholesterol-lowering properties and don't want to take raw or cooked garlic, use the commercial product you find most agreeable.

MAKING YOUR OWN

The very best products in terms of strength, quality, and expense are those you make yourself. Making your own removes any guesswork about the strength of the medicine, and you can make forms more effective than any available commercially. Before using any of the homemade preparations here, be sure to read Chapter 13 on garlic's side effects. Garlic can cause skin burns, and the preparations here that go directly on the skin or in any orifice could cause them.

Allicin in Homemade Products

As we have seen, cutting garlic sets off a biochemical reaction that produces allicin, which gives cut garlic its sharp, biting taste and which has strong antibiotic properties. Over the next twenty-four hours at room temperature, the allicin begins to form a number of other compounds, all of which also have medicinal properties. By the end of a day or two, all the allicin is converted to its by-products. This means that by making your own forms, you can prevent exposure of the product to allicin-destroying heat used in some commercial processes.

- Crush the cloves, mix them with a liquid, and use them immediately for very high allicin content.
- Let crushed or blended cloves sit in water, vinegar, or wine for three to six hours to create a "soup" of many garlic constituents, including much of the original allicin. In many of the recipes following, you'll see I recommend waiting from three hours to overnight before using the preparation.
- Let them soak and age for two or three days to eliminate the allicin and many of the irritating effects of garlic, without the high heat used in commercial oils that yield similar end products. The three-day-old brew is fresher and more potent than anything available in the store.

• Soak crushed cloves in oil to yield constituents not present in raw garlic or in most commercial products.

• Make your own powder with low-temperature drying of garlic slices, ensuring a high allicin content. This homemade powder can be put in gelatin capsules or made into honey pills.

Chest Plaster

Blend five to eight bulbs of garlic. Spread this as a layer on a piece of cheesecloth, and place it, cloth-side down, on the chest. Cover with a heavier cloth, and then with blankets. Put a hot water bottle on top of the poultice under the blankets for added effect. This is a traditional remedy for chest colds, bronchitis, or pneumonia. Don't leave this in place for more than twenty minutes, and remember that some skin is very sensitive to garlic.

Chest Rub

Separate the cloves from a bulb of garlic, chop them up in a blender with a whole onion, and wrap the resulting mixture in a piece of cheesecloth. The cheesecloth will get soaked in the garlic oils. With the garlic still inside, massage the chest with the garlic-moist cloth.

Compress (Cold)

Blend three garlic cloves in a quart of cold water. Dip a cloth in this and put on the affected area. Let it stay in place until the heat of the body warms it up, usually about fifteen minutes. Repeat if desired. This is a great treatment for sunburn. You may also make a cold compress from cold garlic vinegar, described below. For a small compress, soak a cotton ball in garlic infusion, oil, or vinegar, and hold it in place with a Band-Aid or tape.

Compress (Hot)

A compress has many of the benefits of a poultice, but it is less irritating. The water of a compress can also penetrate into areas that a poultice can't reach, such as between the toes or into the cracks of a fungal infection.

Blend three to six cloves of garlic in a pint of hot water. Add this to a pint of boiling water, turn off the heat, and let it cool for a few minutes to a tolerable temperature. Soak a cloth in this, and apply directly over the area to be treated. Add more hot garlic-water to the cloth from time to time to keep it hot and wet. This may be especially effective for a fungal infection. The antibiotic and antifungal properties of garlic are lost within twenty minutes at high heat, so use it as soon as possible after adding it to the boiling water.

A Connoisseur's Garlic Cocktail

Different solvents extract and promote specific chemical reactions among the constituents of garlic. Water, vinegar, alcohol, and oil each draw specific constituents out. Alcohol and water, for instance, is the best solvent to extract allicin. Soaking crushed garlic in oil promotes the production of ajoenes and dithiins, important blood-thinning constituents of garlic. Note that ajoene does not exist in raw garlic but is produced from allicin after garlic is cut. My garlic "cocktail," then, is as follows.

Three cloves of garlic
1 tablespoons red wine
1 tablespoons vinegar
1 tablespoons olive oil

Blend well in a blender. Add one-quarter cup hot water. Let stand for 3 hours. Do not strain. Add one-third of this to a cup of hot water. Take another dose every 3–6 hours until it is all gone.

On paper, this sounds a little like drinking salad dressing, but I find this to be a pleasant and stimulating tonic with a sharp taste. Raw garlic cloves upset my intestines, but this does not.

Cooked Garlic

Cooked garlic is quite effective as a circulatory tonic. In fact, garlic's blood-thinning properties were first discovered in residents of India who took it cooked in their food. Some researchers think that cooking or heating forms new beneficial constituents in garlic that reduce the body's allergic reactions and pain response. The most traditional way to take cooked garlic is fried. Chop the garlic finely, and saute in a small amount of oil. After two minutes or so, add vegetables or other ingredients of a stir-fry, and cook lightly.

Decoction

Blend or finely chop three cloves of garlic, and simmer in a covered pan on the lowest possible heat for twenty minutes. Keep covered and let sit until room temperature. This heating transforms all the allicin in the garlic into its sulfur-containing by-products. This reduces irritation. Some researchers say that boiling garlic creates the set of sulfur compounds that can dilate the bronchi in asthmatic individuals and act as a decongestant, cough medicine, and mucus regulator. A garlic decoction is a traditional treatment for asthma.

Douche

Blend three cloves of garlic very well in three pints of warm water. Strain through clean cloth. Add two tablespoons of apple cider vinegar. Retain the douche for twenty minutes if possible.

Enema

Blend two cloves of garlic in warm water. Administer with a bulb syringe for children. Dr. Chris Deatherage of Missouri says this will clear up pinworms with one or two treatments. It is also useful for influenza and fevers. The garlic constituents are absorbed directly into the bloodstream.

Foot Poultice

Place skinned garlic bulbs in a hot washcloth, and crush well. Lightly oil the bottom of the feet with olive or almond oil. Place the washcloth poultices over the bottom of each foot, and cover each with a sock. Add a hot-water bottle, hot wet compress, or massage the feet vigorously for stronger action. In ten to fifteen minutes, the feet will feel hot, and the acrid scent of garlic will appear in the throat, as the garlic constituents are absorbed through the skin and excreted through the lungs. Remove within twenty-five minutes to prevent burning the skin. Be cautious about skin burns from this treatment.

Foot Bath

Blend up to six cloves in a pint of hot water, and let it sit for an hour. Put the feet in a small tub large enough to cover the feet up to the ankles, in water as hot as you can stand it. Add the blended garlic cloves and water. Add more hot water as necessary to keep the bath hot. Soak the feet for fifteen minutes. This will treat fungal infections and also the entire system, much like a foot poultice. This is an excellent tonic treatment for fatigue.

Infusion

Blend or chop three cloves of garlic. Put in the bottom of a quart canning jar, and add a pint of hot (not boiling) water. Cover with an airtight lid, and let sit overnight or until it reaches room temperature. Strain the liquid. Use within twelve hours.

Inhaler

Crush a clove of garlic and wrap inside a small piece of cotton cloth or cheesecloth. Hold it under the nostrils for sinus infections, head colds, or bronchitis. The aromatic sulfurous substances penetrate into all areas of the upper respiratory tract.

Juice

Juice a bulb of garlic in a centrifugal juicer. Chop the cloves well (it's OK to leave the skins in the chopped-up mash). Drink it immediately, either straight or mixed with carrot juice. Let the juice age for three days to reduce irritating properties.

Nose Drops

Crush some garlic to obtain the juice, or use a centrifugal juicer. Add ten parts water and mix well. Use this as nose drops to prevent colds and flu during epidemics. This is a remedy from rural China.

Oil #1

Blend three to eight entire garlic bulbs in a blender. Chop them well if you don't have a blender. Put the blended garlic in a quart jar and cover with olive oil. Shake it well. Keep it in a warm place for three days, turning the jar from time to time to mix the oil and the garlic. Strain through a cloth. Store in a cool place. Garlic oil is great for earaches. Be sure to warm the oil before putting it in the ear. The oil can also be used to taste on salads or stir-fries (add after cooking).

Oil #2

As above, blend three to eight garlic bulbs in a blender. Cover with almond oil. Let it sit as above in a warm place for three days. Strain through cloth and add one-third part of glycerine (available from a pharmacy). Store in a cool place.

Oil Spread

In the evening, chop one or two garlic cloves with parsley, then crush the mixture with a fork or the edge of a knife. Add enough olive oil to cover it. The next morning for breakfast spread the resulting paste on bread as if it were butter. Sitting overnight in the oil reduces some of the sharp taste.

Poultice #1

For a small poultice, first put petroleum jelly or oil lightly on the area to be treated, to reduce the likelihood of irritation. Place well-crushed garlic on a piece of gauze and put it directly on the skin. Hold it in place with tape or a Band-Aid. Cover with a hot wet cloth, keeping it hot as necessary, for stronger action. Remove after fifteen to twenty minutes. Caution: If left in place too long, this can blister the skin. For longer-term application, try a cold compress of garlic oil or vinegar (see also Foot Poultice on page 193).

Poultice #2

For a larger area, chop an appropriate amount of garlic. Place it on half of a washcloth or dish towel. Fold the other half over it. Crush the garlic thoroughly inside the cloth. Open the cloth and spread the garlic evenly in the center, and place this over the area to be treated, with the garlic against the skin. Hold in place with a bandage or tape. Cover with a hot water bottle or heating pad for stronger action. Never leave in place more than twenty minutes.

Poultice #3

Chop the garlic and mix it with dried chamomile flowers. Add a little hot water as necessary to hold the herbs together. Spread this directly on the area to be treated, cover with a cloth, and secure in place. This poultice is not as irritating as straight garlic. Apply heat for stronger action. Remove in fifteen to twenty minutes.

Raw Garlic

Raw, chopped or crushed garlic is the strongest form available. Some ways to take it, ranging from hot to mild, are:

- Chew up a clove and swallow it.
- Blend a clove in a cup of water or milk and drink it.
- Blend it in one-half cup of carrot juice.
- Blend it in a small amount of aloe vera gel.
- Put the chopped or crushed clove in a cup of already cooked soup or rice, and eat it.
- Try Dr. Subhuti Dharmananda's recipe for raw garlic: Squeeze the juice of one lemon; peel and cut in half three large or five small cloves of garlic, and combine this and the lemon with one cup of water, add a little powdered or fresh ginger and some honey, and blend it until the garlic has been pulverized. Drink the whole thing at once.

Sitz Bath

Blend or finely chop a bulb of garlic and pour a quart of boiling water over it. Let it stand for several hours or until it is at room temperature. Find a tub just big enough to sit in. Fill it with enough hot water to cover you just up to the hips, submerging the anal and genital areas. Add the quart of garlic water, along with the blended garlic. Sit in it for ten minutes. This treatment may be helpful for hemorrhoids, vaginal infections, or other skin problems in the genital area.

Steam

Blend a half bulb of garlic, or chop and crush it as thoroughly as possible. Place in a bowl, and pour a pint of boiling water over it. Cover with a bath towel, and put your head under the towel to inhale the steam. Be careful not to burn yourself!

Suppository #1

Peel the paper-like skin off a clove of garlic. Be careful not to nick the clove, which can release irritating substances. Coat the clove in olive oil and insert it in the vagina or rectum. Keep in place overnight while sleeping.

Suppository #2

Prepare the garlic clove as above, but wrap it in gauze dipped in olive oil. Secure the gauze with thread, and thread a tail on it, like a tampon. This may be more convenient than suppository #1 for vaginal use.

Suppository #3

Mix powdered garlic with melted cocoa butter until it has a thick mud-like consistency. Let it cool in the refrigerator.

Press or roll it into a sheet one-quarter to one-eighth inch thick. Cut into thin strips about one inch long. The final product should be about as big around as a cigarette and about a third as long. Store in the refrigerator, but let it warm to room temperature before use. Once the suppository is inserted, the cocoa butter melts with the body heat, releasing the garlic.

Syrup #1

Chop, slice, or blend ten to twelve garlic bulbs at a time (use a food processor if you like). Place the garlic in thin layers in a jar, alternating it with layers of sugar. Fill up a half gallon jar with the layers. Let this steep for two days. You'll find that the sugar pulls the fluid right out of the garlic. No added liquid is necessary. Strain the juice through a cloth. This syrup is excellent for coughs, bronchitis, congestion in the lungs, colds, sore throats, laryngitis, hoarseness, etc.

Syrup #2

Chop or slice several bulbs of garlic, and place it in a clean glass jar. Cover with local raw unheated honey. Within a day the juice from the garlic will mix with the honey. Take the resulting runny syrup by the teaspoonful every half hour to hour for coughs, sore throats, or congestion in the lungs.

Tincture

Finely chop a bulb of garlic and place it in a pint of grain alcohol, vodka, brandy, gin, or other high-alcohol liquor. Cover and let it steep for two to three weeks, turning and mixing it two or three times a day. Strain and store. The dose is thirty to sixty drops.

Vinegar

Peel, chop, and crush a bulb of garlic, and put it in a quart of either red wine or cider vinegar. Let it sit for a week or two, and strain through cloth.

Wine

Blend one to three garlic cloves in three-fourths of a cup of wine. Let it stand three hours. Take tablespoon doses for a cold or flu or other infection every few hours. This was the antibiotic used by the Roman physician Galen to moisten the bandages of wounded gladiators and disinfect their wounds.

THE BOTTOM LINE ON FORMS

My recommendation on forms is to take them all! Eat cooked garlic regularly and raw garlic occasionally. Take fresh or briefly aged garlic at the first sign of a cold and throughout its course. Take garlic foot baths, compresses, and plasters for acute illnesses or infections. Make garlic vinegars, wines, and syrups, and use them with food or take them as tonics. If you have any disease related to atherosclerosis. or you have cancer or are at risk for any of these, take garlic every day, the equivalent of a half to a whole clove minimum. The commercial forms might be easier to tolerate, but continue to take the other forms in your diet!

CHAPTER 15

GARLIC FOR SPECIFIC DISEASES

In this chapter, I'll explain how to use garlic for a wide variety of diseases. First, a word about the proper boundaries of medical self-care is in order. For any condition with persistent symptoms, you should see a physician. In the Appendix, I give resources to help you find a physician who will use natural methods and herbs if that is what you want. Under no circumstances should you use this book or these recommendations in place of the advice of a qualified doctor. Also read Chapter 13 on the side effects and contraindications of garlic. Garlic can cause serious skin burns, so be cautious when using garlic on the skin or in any body orifice. Don't leave raw garlic or garlic juice in contact with the skin for more than twenty to twenty-five minutes.

THE MEDICINAL ACTIONS OF GARLIC

The following actions of garlic have been demonstrated in either traditional medicine or in modern clinical trials.

- Anti-asthmatic: Eases constricted breathing in asthma
- Anti-epileptic: Reduces frequency or severity of convulsions
- Antiseptic: Fights infection, especially in the digestive and respiratory tracts
- Antispasmodic: Combats cramping and spasmodic pains, especially in the digestive tract
- Anthelmintic: Kills intestinal worms
- Aphrodisiac: Stimulates sexual desire
- Carminative: Helps expel gas
- Diaphoretic: Promotes sweating and circulation to the skin
- Digestive: Stimulates digestion
- Disinfectant: Directly kills germs
- Diuretic (mild): Promotes urination
- Emmenagogue: Promotes menstruation
- Expectorant: Promotes the flow of mucous, improving the productivity of coughs
- Rubefacient: Irritating to the skin, and thus will draw blood supply to an area of the body when applied over that area
- Stimulant: Increases short-term energy
- Tonic: Improves overall health and strength when taken regularly

ABDOMINAL INFLAMMATION

Any persistent or severe abdominal pain requires a visit to the doctor for a diagnosis. For a minor stomachache, try this treatment with garlic: Crush three cloves together with some salt. Pour boiling water over the mixture and let stand until at room temperature. Take the water twice a day for three days.

ACNE

People with persistent acne are often given long-term prescriptions for antibiotics. These are inappropriate for acne, most of which is only accompanied by the normal skin bacteria that is naturally present on the face. Long-term antibiotic prescriptions can wreak havoc with the balance of normal bacteria in the intestines and can create health problems that can last for years. Dietary changes are the first order for acne—less fat, meat, and rich food in the diet, and more fruits and vegetables. Garlic applications to the face have multiple actions that can help acne.

- Garlic is a topical antibiotic
- It increases circulation to the skin
- It is drying

I prefer mild garlic treatments such as a compress over strong ones like a poultice. Garlic is not the best herb for internal treatment of acne. Acne is usually caused by *hot* systemic conditions, to use the terminology of traditional medicine. Cooling herbs such as dandelion, burdock root, or Oregon grape root are better for the internal treatment of acne than garlic.

AIDS

AIDS is considered incurable by conventional medicine, although some individuals remain alive many years after acquiring the HIV virus. Some researchers are currently looking at these survivors to see what they can learn from them in terms of lifestyle, diet, or even genetics that may give a clue to a cure or to better treatment of AIDS. Meanwhile, most therapy aims at prolonging life and at treating the opportunistic infections that AIDS patients are prone to. Garlic appears to have a place in treating such infections as well as improving the overall health of AIDS patients.

Normally, when a new AIDS therapy shows promise in a clinical trial, news spreads quickly in the media. This was unfortunately not the case after a dramatic, although small, trial of garlic for AIDS was reported at the International AIDS Conference in 1989. The researchers, who later published the information in *Deutsche Zeitschrift Onkologie* (German Journal of Oncology) gave an aged garlic preparation (Kyolic garlic) to ten patients with AIDS. All patients had severely low natural killer cell activity and abnormal helper-to-suppressor T-cell ratios—both of these are blood measurements of progressed AIDS, often indicating short life expectancy. All patients also had opportunistic infections such as cryptosporidial diarrhea or herpes infections.

The patients received the equivalent of two cloves a day (5 grams) for the first six weeks, and then the equivalent of four cloves (10 grams) for another six weeks. Three of the patients were too severely ill to complete the trial; they could not complete the garlic regimen and died before the trial ended.

The results were dramatic, and had a pharmaceutical drug been involved instead of garlic, no doubt the news would have spread rapidly in the media. Six of the seven who completed the trial had normal natural killer cell activity within six weeks, and all seven had normal activity by the end of the twelve weeks (natural killer cell activity is considered one of the most important indicators of the progression of AIDS). The helper-to-suppressor T-cell ratios returned to normal in three of the patients, improved in two, remained the same in one, and lowered in one.

Just as important, the patients' opportunistic infections also improved. Chronic diarrhea, candida infection, genital herpes, and a chronic sinus infection all improved. The patient with the chronic sinus infection had gained no relief from antibiotics during more than a year of treatment before the garlic trial.

Exactly why the garlic helped the patients so dramatically is not clearly understood. As we discussed in Chapter 8, garlic can affect the immune system in many ways. Garlic may have also strengthened immunity in these patients by helping to fight the opportunistic infections, thus reducing the load on the immune system. Various trials have shown garlic to be effective against cryptococcus, cryptosporidia, herpes, mycobacteria, and pneumocystis, all common infectious agents in AIDS. Researchers have also recently found evidence that the garlic constituent ajoene may directly interfere with the spread of the HIV virus in AIDS patients.

This trial was small, with only seven patients completing it, and follow-up studies are necessary to prove that garlic will really help AIDS patients. News of the trial spread like wildfire in the AIDS community, however, and many patients now take garlic regularly. One study in 1993 found that nearly 10 percent of AIDS patients surveyed took garlic supplements in addition to the other medications they were taking.

Garlic is used routinely in the Healing Aids Research Project at Bastyr University in Seattle. This is one of the few medical centers doing formal research into natural treatments of AIDS. Dr. Jane Guiltinan, medical director of the clinic where the research is done, suggests that all AIDS patients who can tolerate garlic should take it. "I most often prescribe garlic in food form rather than capsules or extracts," says Guiltinan. "I have them eat as much as possible, either raw or cooked."

AIDS patients might take garlic in any of its oral forms, use garlic poultices, compresses, or oil for skin afflictions, enemas for anal infections, or steams or chest applications for sinus or bronchial problems.

APPETITE LOSS

Most of us think of garlic as a food spice rather than as a medicinal herb. Cascade Anderson Geller, my herbal teacher at National College of Naturopathic Medicine in Portland, Oregon, corrected me one day when I made a distinction between herbs and food spices. "Spices *are* herbs," she said simply. I soon came to understand that adding spices to food is our most common use of herbs, and that increasing appetite and improving digestion is one of the most important treatments in natural medicine. Every cell and enzyme system in the body is built up with the food we eat, and if digestion is deficient or unbalanced, there will be corresponding deficiency or imbalance in the body. We usually feel this first as low energy and fatigue.

Appetite loss is an important first warning sign from the body that something is going wrong. Acutely it usually means it's time for a short fast to give the system a rest. But chronic poor appetite invites stimulation and warming of the digestive system, and we have few medicines available for this as valuable as garlic. In a Japanese clinical trial of patients with vague complaints, including poor appetite, garlic supplements improved the appetite in most of the patients. Take garlic freely in the diet and also take a teaspoon of garlic vinegar or wine before meals. If the garlic causes much irritation and feeling of heat rather than pleasant stimulation and warmth, try cooling bitter herbs such as gentian or Oregon grape root instead. Take them twenty minutes before meals.

ARTHRITIS

Garlic is not appropriate for *internal* use for rheumatoid arthritis, which is a very hot condition by nature. The garlic can make the pain of a flare-up worse. Osteoarthritis, which is possibly due to wear and tear on the joints as we age, is usually a cold condition by nature, and garlic may be helpful internally, but use caution if pain is severe, and stop immediately if the garlic seems to make it worse. Use cooked garlic and onions, which have anti-inflammatory properties only when heated. Ginger in the diet also has a strong anti-inflammatory effect, as much as some prescription anti-inflammatory drugs. Garlic decoction may also be helpful for osteoarthritis as it is for asthma.

Garlic is appropriate for *external* use in arthritis as a counterirritant. Use a poultice for up to twenty minutes directly over the painful spot, and apply heat over it. The garlic and the heat draw healing circulation to the area. If the pain worsens, then try another treatment besides garlic. Homeopathy has also been proven in clinical trials to help rheumatoid arthritis.

ASTHMA

Ancient Egyptians and Romans and medieval Arabs and Persians all used garlic to treat asthma. An angel appeared to the abbess of a twelfth-century German monastery and told her how to treat asthma with a garlic tea, and the use entered into European monastic medicine. Even conventional physicians in Germany and the United States used garlic for asthma in the first half of the twentieth century. The biochemical mechanism involved may be that garlic affects substances called prostaglandins in the body. Garlic must be cooked or heated to have this benefit. Here's the recipe that the angel told to Hildegard von Bingen, the German abbess:

> Finely chop two garlic cloves, add a handful of hyssop leaves (available at a health food store or herb store), and simmer on low heat in a quart of water for twenty to thirty minutes. Drink a cup as needed.

Contemporary British herbalists use a tincture of garlic with coltsfoot and lobelia for asthma.

ATHEROSCLEROSIS/CORONARY ARTERY DISEASE

We see in Chapter 9 that garlic is an effective circulatory tonic. It is used for atherosclerosis or "hardening of the arteries" at least since the time of the Greeks. Conventional physicians in Germany use garlic both to prevent and to treat atherosclerosis and coronary artery disease. (See also "Heart Attack" and "Claudication" in this chapter.) For this purpose, you'll need to take garlic regularly, at least a clove a day either raw or cooked. For prevention, lower doses are effective, as low as 600 to 900 milligrams of powder a day (one-fourth to one-third of a clove).

BITES AND STINGS

Garlic probably appears as a treatment for bites and stings of snakes, scorpions, insects, and wild animals more than for any other purpose around the world. Apply crushed garlic to the bite. In Arabia and India, the garlic is chewed up, mixed with spittle, and placed directly on the wound. Also take some internally. For animal bites, a garlic wash is great for first aid. Blend up some cloves in warm water. Wash the wound with it thoroughly, and then keep a moist compress on it. Of course you should seek medical treatment for serious bites and stings.

BLOOD CLOTS

Garlic has blood-thinning properties and can be a useful addition to conventional treatments to prevent blood clots. Blood-thinning drugs are often prescribed after strokes, heart attacks, or blood clots in the legs or lungs. *Important*: Consult your physician if you are taking these drugs and want to take anything more than a moderate dietary amount of garlic. Garlic can interfere with these drugs by making them more potent, and the side effects from improper doses of blood-thinning drugs are already a common cause of hospital admissions.

BOILS

In a comedy by the ancient Greek Aristophanes, a character limping awkwardly in a pair of new boots is asked if he is using a garlic poultice to cure a boil on his foot. Garlic is used exactly this way today in the popular medicine of Guangxi province in China. Treat a boil with external applications of garlic. A poultice is best. Be careful not to cause garlic burns on the tissues around the boil. Boils are usually a sign of a hot systemic condition, so take cooling herbs like dandelion root, burdock, or Oregon grape root. I get frequent boils, and I treat them externally with a garlic poultice for twenty minutes, and internally with a tea of half burdock and half stinging nettle leaf.

BRONCHITIS

Bronchitis with congestion is one of the "sure bets" for garlic treatment. The garlic is an expectorant, promoting the secretion of healing mucous, and it is also an antibiotic. After garlic enters the body, either through digestion or through absorption through the skin in a poultice, some of its constituents are excreted through the lungs. These sulfur-containing volatile substances are antibiotic and antiseptic, and thus garlic treats bronchial and lung conditions from the inside out.

My brother used to suffer from chronic bronchitis. After years of antibiotic treatments, he gradually developed allergies to each of the antibiotics he received, including amoxycillin, erythromycin, sulfa, and tetracycline. One day, his doctor told him: "You're on your own. I don't have any more antibiotics I can give you." He began treating himself with garlic and ginger. He would eat a clove or two of garlic every day and eat a slice of fresh ginger every few hours and take a cup of ginger tea in the evening. He minced the garlic cloves and put one or two in a little olive oil. He "nuked" these for ten seconds in the microwave to reduce some of the sharp taste, and put a spoonful in the back of his throat and swallowed it. He would also add a clove to stir-fries or other foods when appropriate. His bronchitis gradually got better, and within six months he didn't have it anymore. Now whenever he feels a recurrence coming on, he starts the garlic again and some ginger tea.

For powerful direct treatments of acute bronchitis, try a garlic steam, foot poultice, foot bath, or compress or poultice to the chest over the affected area. The foot treatments supply sulfur constituents to the system right through the skin, and they are excreted through the lungs within fifteen to twenty minutes.

CANCER

If you or someone close to you has cancer or are at risk of getting cancer, read Chapter 10 in detail to see how garlic may help you. Garlic supports several mechanisms of anti-cancer activity in the body. Of course it is not a treatment for cancer by itself, but it makes a good adjunct to other treatments, whether conventional or alternative. Several studies have shown that garlic can reduce the side effects of chemotherapy and radiation therapy.

CANDIDA

Candida albicans is a yeast that occurs naturally in the digestive tract, on the skin, and in the vagina. When the body's immune system or natural balance of healthy bacteria becomes disrupted, often through abuse of antibiotics, a candida overgrowth can occur. Some doctors think that mild candida overgrowth in the intestines can be responsible for a systemic yeast syndrome accompanied by multiple allergies, chronic fatigue, and mental and emotional complaints.

Garlic is an effective antibiotic against candida albicans, and a direct application to infected areas in the form of a poultice, compress, douche, or enema can be very effective. Garlic in any of the internal forms in Chapter 14 can help systemic candida, through garlic's immune-enhancing and tonic effects.

You can treat oral thrush, a candida yeast infection in the mouth in some children, as well as in adult AIDS patients, with garlic oil. Simply rub the garlic oil into the infected area. The oil does not have the irritating effects of raw garlic.

CHEMOTHERAPY/RADIOTHERAPY

Garlic may help prevent some of the symptoms and side effects of chemotherapy and radiation treatments. These treatments are given to kill cancer cells, but they also attack many other cells in the body. In a Japanese clinical trial, one group of women receiving chemotherapy of radiation therapy also received garlic treatments. Those patients who took the garlic had fewer side effects than those who did not. See Chapter 10 for more about garlic, cancer, and chemotherapy.

CLAUDICATION

Intermittent claudication is a painful condition of the legs and buttocks that makes walking difficult. It is one of the signs of atherosclerosis, a narrowing of the arteries. The arteries in the lower truck or legs become partially blocked, and blood supply to the muscles of the legs is reduced. This greatly restricts the distance a person can walk until the muscles are exhausted and pain and cramping sets in. In a clinical trial of garlic in claudication, garlic significantly improved the maximum distance the patients could walk. The effects started after about five weeks of continuous administration. The scientists conducting the trial state that the improvement is probably due to garlic's blood-thinning properties, which also require four to six weeks to take effect. It appears that the thinner blood was better able to circulate through the narrowed arteries.

Dr. R. F. Weiss of Germany, author of the standard medical text on plant medicine there, says that many serious cases were completely relieved with garlic therapy, even when all other treatments had failed.

COMMON COLD

In a clinical trial in Japan, patients with the common cold or viral bronchitis received garlic, and improvement in symptoms was monitored. At the end of the trial, almost 90 percent of participants judged the garlic to be effective in reducing fatigue, aching muscles, and respiratory symptoms.

Many patients request antibiotic prescriptions from their doctors for colds and flu. Antibiotics are not appropriate, however, because they have no effect against the viruses that cause these conditions. Unfortunately, many doctors comply with patients' wishes, even though it is against their medical training to do so. They reason that if the patients want the drugs, they will go elsewhere to get them anyway. Antibiotics have many possible side effects and can cause chronic conditions to worsen.

If you have a cold or flu and want antibiotics, try garlic instead. Garlic has direct effects against viruses as well as bacteria. More important, it activates the immune system's own efforts against these invaders. It is also an expectorant and will help clear mucous membranes of congestion. Take garlic in one of its many raw forms, and take it in higher doses. My favorite cold treatment: Blend three garlic cloves in one-half cup of carrot juice and swallow the whole thing down. Do this three times a day. Make a soup of garlic, onions, and greens and have that in place of a meal. Try a garlic foot bath twice a day, or a garlic steam. Garlic syrup is also helpful for colds accompanied by cough or sore throat. Be sure to drink plenty of liquids along with the garlic, because it can be overly drying.

If you have a very high fever (above 102°F) or are dehydrated, try more cooling herbs such as echinacea. More than ten thousand people, many of them elderly, die of the flu each year in the United States One common cause of death is dehydration accompanying prolonged flu, so be sure to avoid medicinal amounts of garlic if you are thirsty and dehydrated. If your cold or flu persists more than three or four days, be sure to consult a physician.

Constipation

Laxative dependence is one of the most common forms of herbal abuse in the United States. A person taking herbal or commercial laxatives containing herbs such as *cascara sagrada* eventually requires the product to have a normal bowel movement. For chronic constipation—moderate exercise, drinking more liquids, and eating more whole grains, fresh fruits, and vegetables will help. Bulk herbal laxatives like psyllium seed are more appropriate than stimulating laxatives like cascara sagrada.

Garlic may also have a place in chronic constipation because poor digestion and unbalanced intestinal bacteria commonly cause constipation, and garlic can help these. After correcting the lifestyle factors above, try a three-day treatment with raw garlic as if you were treating an intestinal infection (three to six cloves of fresh crushed garlic in one of the forms in Chapter 14 for three days). Then take garlic in moderate amounts, one-half to one clove a day regularly for four to eight weeks.

In a clinical trial of more than a thousand Japanese patients who all suffered from fatigue and other vague complaints, eight weeks of treatment with garlic and vitamins brought about improvement in most of them. One of the symptoms that responded best was constipation.

CORNS

Here is a corn treatment from China:

Crush equal amounts of garlic and onions into a paste. Clean the area around the corn and disinfect it with alcohol. Trim it down with a knife as far as possible but not deep enough to make it bleed. Soak the foot in salt water. In about twenty minutes, the corn becomes soft. Moisten the garlic-onion paste with vinegar. Put this directly on the corn, and cover it with a bandage. Leave on for twenty minutes. Repeat the process every other day. The corn will usually heal within a week.

COUGHS

Residents of ancient India, Greece, Rome, China, Arabia, Medieval Europe, sixteenth-century England and Germany, colonial United States and Mexico, and even nineteenth- and twentieth-century physicians in the United States have all used garlic as a cough remedy. A common thread throughout many of these treatments is that the garlic is made into a cough syrup with either sugar or honey. See the recipes in Chapter 14 for two ways to make a garlic cough syrup. In addition to stimulating the congested mucous membranes, garlic promotes the immune system's efforts to fight off any infection involved.

DENTAL PROBLEMS

In the days of modern dentistry, we don't usually have to deal with broken or rotten teeth ourselves. If you ever have such a dental emergency, you can crush garlic and disinfect the tooth with it directly. The ancient Greeks would mix it with frankincense for this purpose. Ancient Egyptians filled hollow teeth with garlic and honey to prevent abscesses.

DIABETES

Garlic or its constituents have been found in a handful of scientific trials to lower blood sugar. Thus it may be helpful for diabetics. A word of caution here: Some diabetics hope that they may be able to control the disease with natural remedies. Usually they hope to be able to avoid the restrictive diabetic diet. In a few mild cases this may be possible, under the supervision of a physician trained in natural medicine *(see your telephone directory for finding a physician who utilizes herbal therapies)*. Many herbs do, in fact, have blood sugar-lowering or insulin-like effects. But patients should not get their hopes too high for controlling diabetes completely with herbs, including garlic. R. F. Weiss, M.D., the master physician and herbalist who wrote the standard German medical-level herbal textbook *Lehrbuch der Phytotherapie*, cautions against relying on antidiabetic teas and herbs. Weiss saw, again and again, the failure of such treatments, usually with serious complications for the patient, including the nerve damage characteristic of the disease. He suggests that patients should rely mainly on diet and insulin to control diabetes, take blood sugar-lowering medications only as much as necessary, and use herbs only as an adjunct to dietary control.

Most research into the blood sugar-lowering effects of garlic have been done on isolated constituents rather than garlic itself. The constituents studies have included allicin, allyl propyl disulfide, and S-allyl cysteine sulfoxide. Garlic constituents appear to act by blocking the inactivation of insulin in the liver. The result is higher blood insulin levels and lower blood sugar. There's no solid research indicating that garlic is a practical treatment for diabetics, however, if taken regularly.

One case study indicates how garlic might be helpful. The patient, as reported by Georg Madaus in his German botanical text *Lerhbuch der Bioligischen Heilmittel*, was taking 100 cc of insulin a day, but still had a blood sugar count of 242 milligrams and urinary sugar of 8 percent. After taking six garlic capsules a day for a week, the blood sugar had fallen to 215 milligrams and the urinary sugar to 2 percent. Notice that the garlic was used *in addition to* conventional therapy, not in place of it.

Garlic is probably contraindicated for self-medication in patient with brittle diabetes. The blood sugar in this condition can make wild swings from high to low. Consult your doctor before taking garlic in medicinal amounts if you have this condition.

Garlic has perhaps a better use for diabetics than lowering blood sugar. It prevents atherosclerosis, which is a common complication of diabetes. Diabetics can add the equivalent of a clove of garlic a day to their diet in any form they like, i.e., cooked in food, garlic wine, capsules, etc.

DIARRHEA AND DYSENTERY

Garlic is such a good preventive or treatment for "traveler's diarrhea" that I never travel to foreign countries without taking six or eight bulbs with me. Each evening, crush three cloves in a cup of hot water. Drink the water the next day in three divided doses. Diarrhea is a common response to exposure to unfamiliar bacteria in a new area. If you actually get diarrhea, eat two or three of the cloves raw during the day. You might also try activated charcoal for diarrhea, available at pharmacies in capsules. My traveler's kit includes garlic bulbs, echinacea tincture, sedative herbs to help sleep, activated charcoal tablets, and French green cosmetic clay to make poultices for bites or stings.

Garlic is used throughout the third-world countries to prevent or treat dysentery. It has direct antibiotic actions against a number of bacteria and parasites that can cause serious cases of dysentery, which can cause death. Researchers in India tested garlic in rabbits with induced dysentery from the *Shigella* bacterium. Within an hour of taking the extracts, the rabbits' blood serum showed activity against the bacteria. By the second day of treatment, rectal swabs of the rabbits showed none of the bacteria present. All the rabbits were cured within three days. In the control group, which did not take garlic, four of the five rabbits died within forty-eight hours.

EAR PROBLEMS, DEAFNESS

Childhood ear infections are the most common cause for a visit to the doctor among children aged one to six years.

Unfortunately, these are often treated with antibiotics, which are usually inappropriate because no infectious agent can be found in the ear for many cases. Conventional medical researchers have demonstrated for more than twenty years that antibiotics do no better than simpler treatments for these middle ear problems, but unfortunately the practice continues. Many ear problems are actually due to allergies and to environmental causes such as secondhand cigarette smoke.

For a childhood ear infection, it is important to cut out dairy and mucous-producing foods. Diluted fruit juices and warm vegetable broth should be drunk freely, along with plenty of water. This helps to thin the mucous and ease pain. Nasal decongestants are as effective as antibiotics for relieving the ear pain, according to scientific research. Warm garlic oil, not cold, in the ear can also help (the cold can contract the tissues in the ear, causing increased pain). Some children may find garlic oil irritating, so be prepared to swab it out with a cotton tip if it causes discomfort.

When I first moved to Oregon, with its cool, damp, and moldy climate, I suffered from fungal infections in one ear. Natural treatments such as tea tree oil were of no help. Garlic oil, however, with its warming effects, circulatory stimulation, and direct antifungal action is very effective for this problem.

Warm garlic oil in the ears is also a traditional remedy for deafness in many cultures—see the case study by an Appalachian healer in Chapter 7. It has probably gained this reputation because it can remove built-up ear wax, and it probably has no healing effect of deafness from other causes.

Eczema

Eczema is an allergic skin reaction that can cause severe itching. To relieve the symptoms, try garlic foot or hand baths, cold compresses, or apply garlic juice directly to the area affected. With crushed garlic or garlic juice, be wary of possible inflammation or skin burns in sensitive individuals. If you find garlic irritates the tissues, try a poultice of French green cosmetic clay.

Emphysema/Chronic Obstructive Pulmonary Disease

Emphysema and related conditions are caused by the destruction of lung tissue, and they are not considered curable. The symptoms can be treated and improved, however. The noted French folk herbalist Maurice Mességué recommended the following formula for foot and hand baths for emphysema:

Garlic: one head crushed
Hawthorn flowers: one handful
Sage: one handful
Thyme: one handful

Place these in a quart of lukewarm water and allow to sit for four to five hours. Bottle and store. For a foot or hand bath, boil two quarts of water, turn off the heat, and add a half pint of the liquid prepared above. Take the bath as hot as you can stand. If you have a thermometer, 104 to 110 degrees is the best temperature range. Soak the feet for eight minutes in the morning, before breakfast, and the hands for eight minutes in the evening, before dinner. The bath liquid can be saved, reheated, and reused, but it shouldn't be boiled again or have more water added.

Fatigue (Chronic)

Chronic fatigue is not an illness itself, but it is secondary to many other conditions such as adrenal exhaustion, chronic candida infection, coffee abuse, psychological stress, and so on. First, get a thorough physical examination to determine possible causes. Resist any suggestions by a conventional physician to take antidepressant drugs, which will do nothing to correct the cause of your fatigue. Ultimately the best treatment for chronic fatigue is removal of underlying causes, stress management, counseling, improved diet and lifestyle, better rest and recreation, elimination of stimulants, and introduction of tonic herbs such as licorice, Siberian ginseng, or Chinese ginseng.

Other herbal treatments are usually necessary first, however, to prepare the system for the tonic treatments. If the fatigue is not accompanied by signs of heat, such as hot hands and feet, low-grade fever, and night sweats, try a course of three cloves of garlic, in one of the raw forms in Chapter 14, for a week. If you tolerate the garlic, try taking a whole bulb of it raw on one of those days. Blend it in milk or carrot juice to prevent irritation. This may help clear up any intestinal infections or parasites that may be contributing to the condition. It will also boost the immune system against any infections present. Follow this treatment with a tincture of echinacea and prickly ash bark (you can buy them in a health food store and mix them together). Take 40 to 60 drops three times a day for two weeks. If signs of heat are more prevalent, try taking echinacea in large doses first in place of the garlic—three one-tablespoon doses a day for a week—and then take the echinacea–prickly ash, as listed. After the first week of treatment (garlic or echinacea), take dandelion root or burdock root tea three times a day for three weeks. Throughout this time, take a low-fat, moderate-protein diet with plenty of fresh fruits and vegetables. If you want dairy, take yogurt or butter. If you want meat, take chicken or fish. Only after the treatments with dandelion root or burdock root are complete, start taking licorice root or ginseng root as tonics to boost your energy. It is best to have a physician who practices natural medicine manage a case of chronic fatigue; see the Appendix for a list

In Japan, a group of patients with chronic fatigue and other vague complaints was treated with a simple regimen of a garlic supplement (Kyolic) with vitamins for four to eight weeks. Of all the symptoms measured in the patients, fatigue improved the most. Results were better after eight weeks than after four. See Chapter 11 for more details of this study and for more about the benefits of garlic on stress, fatigue, and aging.

FOOD POISONING

Short-term treatment with garlic is an effective treatment for many cases of nausea from food poisoning or intestinal flu. I suggest it be taken slightly cooked, simmered ten minutes as a tea, rather than raw, to prevent irritation.

I had a patient, an immigrant from Africa, who worked in a fast-food hamburger chain. He was Muslim and had been fasting during the Muslim holy month. Muslims break their fast each evening at sunset after taking no food or water since dawn each day for the month. One day, he was at work and had to break his fast on hamburgers. Either he got some bad hamburger, or it was a poor choice of foods to break his fast with—his stomach and intestines, from fasting, were not ready to take such heavy food. He may have also contracted an intestinal flu. Whatever it was, he spent much of the night vomiting and even considered going to the hospital at one point. Finally, he vomited up something he described as "oily" and felt relief. When he called me on the phone the next day he still felt too sick to eat. I recommended he see a doctor, because of the severity of the symptoms. He was poor, however, and was unwilling to go to the doctor. I made him promise that if he was not better that evening or if the nausea got worse again that he'd see the doctor, which he agreed to. I had to recommend something he had in the house or could get at a nearby store, so I prescribed a tea of three cloves of garlic and an equivalent amount of ginger simmered ten minutes in a quart of water, to be drunk in two divided doses.

This immediately relieved any feeling of queasiness. For the next few days, whenever he ate, he would feel uncomfortably bloated. But if he drank the tea, he would immediately feel better. After a few days, he noticed that the tea started to cause a burning sensation in his stomach, and I had him switch to simple ginger tea without the garlic. This is a common reaction with garlic treatments—that after two to five days it becomes irritating—which demonstrates that garlic in its raw form is typically a short-term medicine for short-term illnesses.

FUNGAL INFECTIONS

Garlic has direct antibiotic effects against funguses such as those that cause athlete's foot or vaginal infections. Any of the direct garlic applications in Chapter 14 may be effective. My favorite for athlete's foot is the garlic foot bath twice a day and garlic oil put directly on the affected area in between. Concentrated garlic preparations, such as garlic juice, may be effective, but they may also irritate the already inflamed tissues.

HANGOVERS

A novel use for garlic, suggested by animal trials, is for hangover. Japanese researchers, testing the ability of garlic to increase resistance to stress, fed alcohol to mice until the animals lost coordination. Mice who received garlic had a quicker recovery from loss of coordination. The alcohol also cleared from their blood faster. The maximum effect for the mice was a dose in the range of 250 to 500 milligrams per kilogram of body weight. That's five to fifteen cloves for the average man. Such a dose could decrease the time to "sober up" after drinking or shorten the duration of a hangover the next day. No doubt ten cloves of raw garlic would be a more effective pick-me-up than another drink in the morning.

HEART ATTACKS

Garlic is not a treatment for heart attack, which is an emergency condition, but research shows that it may prevent a second one if you've had an attack already. Researchers from India at the First World Congress on the Health Significance of Garlic and Garlic Constituents (held in 1990 in Washington, D.C.) described a three-year study among 432 patients who had already suffered one heart attack. One group received daily supplements of garlic juice in milk and the other did not. Those who took the garlic had fewer second heart attacks and also had lower blood pressure and serum cholesterol levels. After three years, about twice as many patients had died in the group not taking garlic. During the study, the benefits of garlic increased steadily with time, suggesting that garlic was actually dissolving the atherosclerotic blockages in coronary arteries. The patients taking garlic also received other benefits, including increased energy and sexual desire, more tolerance for exercise, and a decrease in joint pains and asthma.

Other trials have shown benefits to cooked as well as raw garlic. A group of patients with chest pains due to heart disease took either raw or cooked garlic for a month. Their blood was then tested for its tendency to clot. Both groups had "thinner" blood at the end of a month—a good sign for the prevention of heart attacks. The group taking cooked garlic had almost the same benefits as those taking raw.

If you plan to take medicinal amounts of garlic and you are taking blood-thinning drugs, consult your physician first.

See Chapter 9 for more details about garlic's benefits in cardiovascular disease.

HEAVY-METAL POISONING

The use of garlic to prevent and treat lead poisoning was the discovery of Bulgarian scientist Vesselin Petkov. He conducted many experiments into the traditional uses of garlic in his country. One day he theorized that the detoxifying sulfur-containing compounds in garlic might help treat or prevent lead poisoning. First he tested the theory in rabbits. Garlic nearly doubled the survival rate of rabbits with lead poisoning. He then experimented with workers at a local lead factory. He gave garlic extracts to a group of workers there and found an 83 percent reduction in signs of lead poisoning in them, and in those with lead poisoning, the symptoms were less severe. In two groups of workers who originally had no signs of lead poisoning, 28 percent of the normal group began to develop signs at the end of three months, while only 3 percent of the group taking garlic showed such signs.

Petkov's findings were circulated throughout the Communist world at the time, and garlic supplementation became a standard preventive prescription for lead factory workers in many countries. In lead factories today in China, workers take two cloves of raw garlic twice a day to prevent or treat lead poisoning.

Garlic may also be helpful for other heavy metals besides lead. Dr. Benjamin Lao of the Loma Linda University School of Medicine in California conducted an experiment using garlic extract in a test-tube. He put human blood solutions in test tubes containing lead, mercury, copper, or aluminum. Normally, these metals will cause the destruction of red blood cells. In solutions pretreated with garlic, however, no such destruction occurred. Japanese researchers also demonstrated protection against mercury poisoning in animals, and obtained a patent for a garlic preparation for the same purpose in humans.

HEMORRHOIDS

People of many countries have used garlic as a treatment for hemorrhoids. The simplest method is to insert a whole peeled garlic clove in the rectum. Be careful not to nick the skin of the clove when you are peeling it. See also the other recipes for suppositories in Chapter 14. Another method of treatment is the garlic sitz bath, also described in Chapter 14.

HERPES

Herpes viruses can infect either the genital or oral areas. Garlic may be an effective treatment because of its antiviral and immune-stimulating properties. Use garlic internally at the first sign of an impending outbreak. Then when sores have opened up, treat them with any of the external applications described in Chapter 14. The strongest method is to apply garlic juice directly to the sores, but be careful not to irritate the tissues. For genital herpes, try a twenty-minute garlic sitz bath in hot water.

Dr. Tariq Abdullah, a prominent garlic researcher from the Akbar Clinic and Research Center in Panama City, Florida, said in the August 1987 issue of *Prevention* that he had received reports of patients who could control severe outbreaks of genital herpes by taking garlic orally.

HIGH BLOOD PRESSURE

At least seventeen clinical trials have shown that garlic can lower blood pressure. The drop in blood pressure is only small, five to ten points, with the 600- to 900-milligram doses in most of the trials. One trial showed a larger drop of sixteen points with the equivalent of one clove of garlic a day. For more about garlic and blood pressure, see Chapter 9. Don't expect garlic to lower blood pressure on its own. High blood pressure is nature's way of telling you to exercise, eat more fresh fruits and vegetables, eat less fat and protein, and control your stress levels better. Garlic will help as you make changes in your life, but it won't do the whole job. Take garlic raw if possible, from one to three cloves a day.

HIGH CHOLESTEROL

We saw in great detail in Chapter 9 how garlic can lower cholesterol. If you want to use it for this purpose, the dose is a half to a whole clove of garlic a day or the equivalent. If you don't tolerate garlic well, a dose as low as 600 milligrams of garlic powder in capsules has been effective in clinical trials. Take the garlic for at least three months. Often in the first month or two, the cholesterol and other blood fats will actually rise, so be patient for results.

HOARSENESS

Garlic in any of its raw forms may help hoarseness. If you only have garlic capsules, you'll have to open them up, mix them with a little warm water, and gargle.

INFECTIONS

Take garlic internally at the first sign of infection in a minor cut or wound. Simultaneously use one of the external applications in Chapter 14. See a physician for any serious cut or wound, or if an infection persists. My favorite treatment is to wash the cut with garlic wine, then apply crushed garlic over a garlic-wine soaked gauze pad placed on the wound. Put more cloth over the poultice, and apply heat over the top of this, with a hot-water bottle or with cloth dipped in water as hot as you can stand it. Continue the treatment for fifteen to twenty minutes.

INFLUENZA

We usually think of influenza as a minor illness, but it actually kills more than ten thousand people in the United States each year. Many of its victims are elderly. Twice over the last one hundred years, virulent strains of flu have swept the world in epidemics that killed tens of millions of people each time.

Garlic can be very effective for both treatment and prevention of the flu. At the first sign of an epidemic, as soon as a coworker starts sniffling or the neighbor child is home from school with the flu, increase your intake of garlic. Take it in one of the raw forms in Chapter 14. See also the recipe in Chapter 14 for garlic nose drops, which the Chinese use in times of epidemics.

Garlic acts directly against the influenza virus and also stimulates the body's natural defenses against it. In one animal study, researchers fed a garlic extract to mice and then introduced the flu virus into their nasal passages. All the mice that had received the garlic were protected from the flu, while the untreated animals all got sick (See also "Common Cold" in this chapter).

INSECT BITES

For mosquito bites, bee stings, chiggers, and other insect bites, try a remedy used all across Arabia and India. Chew up a little garlic, mix it well with your spittle, and put it directly on the bite. Hold it in place with a Band-Aid or tape for twenty minutes, keeping watch for any signs of irritation or skin burns.

NICOTINE WITHDRAWAL

Garlic was used by physicians in pre–World War II Germany for treatment of nicotine poisoning. This suggests that it may also be helpful for those quitting smoking. Garlic's detoxifying properties will help clear the nicotine from the system. Its expectorant effects and other beneficial effects on the lungs and bronchial tract can also help heal the tissues there. It may also help the diarrhea or constipation that often accompany withdrawal from nicotine. Try taking it in any form you like from Chapter 14.

NOSEBLEED

The Chinese use garlic in the following way to treat nosebleed. Crush three cloves of garlic and bind them to the center of the foot, on the right foot for the right nostril, or the left foot for the left nostril. The bleeding will stop when the soles of the feet feel very hot.

PARASITES

Intestinal parasites can cause chronic diarrhea, malabsorption of food, and debilitation of the whole system. These parasites are usually picked up while traveling in other countries. Sometimes *giardia* infection is contracted by drinking unpurified water while camping in the United States. AIDS patients also often get parasitic infections. Garlic has antiparasitic effects. Dr. Chris Deatherage of Missouri recommends raw garlic juice for parasites. Any of the raw forms in Chapter 14 may be of benefit.

PERTUSSIS (WHOOPING COUGH)

Pertussis, or whooping cough, has occurred worldwide throughout recorded medical history. Despite intensive vaccination of infants in the United States, the disease in on the rise here. About a fourth of the cases are in adults, who usually have much milder symptoms than young children do. Because adults with mild cases are probably the main carriers of the disease to young children during epidemics, any persistent cough in an adult should be examined by a physician.

Pertussis vaccine is controversial. It is standard in the United States but is banned in some European countries. It can cause neurological damage and convulsions. It has been suggested, but not proven conclusively, that pertussis vaccination may be responsible for some cases of sudden infant death syndrome. Whatever the level of adverse effects to the vaccine, it is unlikely that they approach the severity of the 1 to 2 percent fatality rate for infants under one year of age who contract pertussis.

Children younger than two are at most risk, and the disease is mainly only troublesome for children and adults older than that. At all ages, the disease can be traumatic for patient and caregiver alike. The infection usually lasts six to eight weeks but can last as long as three months, with a two-week period of severe coughing and frequent vomiting.

Pertussis is caused by bacteria. It starts with what appears to be a mild chest cold for one to two weeks. Severe spasmodic coughs come in rapid sequences, five to as many as fifteen in a row, followed by a deep inhalation to catch the breath. The sound of this in-breath is the "whoop" of "whooping cough." Vomiting is also common during this phase. After several more weeks, the coughing becomes milder, but the illness usually persists another few weeks. The biggest risk with pertussis at all ages, and especially among the elderly, is the development of serious complications such as pneumonia.

An infant with pertussis should be hospitalized, because constant nursing attention is necessary and because emergency measures, such as suction to remove mucous obstruction from the throat, or other emergency measures to clear the airway may be necessary. For mild cases without complication in older children, doctors usually offer no treatment. Antibiotics are not effective once the disease has set in. Home care with garlic preparations (after appropriate medical consultation) may improve the comfort and prevent complications. See Chapter 14 for several ways to make a garlic cough syrup.

Garlic has been used in many cultures for whooping cough. It is used that way today in China. Garlic is well suited to whooping cough for several reasons. First, it is a mild expectorant, helping to loosen the persistent mucous that accompanies the disease. Garlic is also antispasmodic and may reduce the severity of the coughing. Finally, and perhaps most importantly, garlic has antibiotic and immune-stimulating properties and can help prevent serious complications like pneumonia.

Contemporary treatment in China, widely used throughout rural areas, and just as likely to be effective here as there, is to take about ten cloves of garlic, remove the skin and crush the cloves thoroughly. Cover with one-half cup of hot water and let it soak for five to six hours. Add sugar to make a syrup. The dose is one-half teaspoonful for a child younger than three years old, and a full teaspoon for a child older than three (three times a day for all children). See also the other recipes for garlic syrup in Chapter 14.

Caution might be in order with garlic if the child has severe vomiting, because such vomiting can be dehydrating, and garlic could aggravate the dehydration. Any signs of dehydration should be addressed by a physician.

STROKE

If you are at risk for a stroke, or if you have already had one, consider taking garlic regularly to thin the blood and prevent clotting. If you are already taking blood-thinning drugs, don't take large amounts of garlic without consulting your doctor, who may want to monitor your drug dose as the garlic begins to thin the blood. Garlic's blood-thinning properties are mostly preserved after cooking, so add garlic to your meals.

TUBERCULOSIS

Most people will never have the need for a home cure for tuberculosis—this serious condition requires medical treatment, and local boards of health keep track of cases to prevent epidemics. However, tuberculosis in on the rise, associated with AIDS and increasing malnutrition in poor areas of the urban United States. Drug-resistant tuberculosis is an increasing problem in some areas. If you or someone you know has drug-resistant tuberculosis, you might try garlic as a treatment. The Chinese treat tuberculosis with garlic in the following way:

> Take a bulb of garlic, separate the cloves, and peel their skins.
>
> Put the garlic in boiling water for sixty seconds only, and then scoop them out of the water.
>
> Add white rice to the water and cook it into a gruel.
>
> Mix the half-cooked garlic cloves back in with the rice gruel and eat the mixture after meals. Do this daily.
>
> In addition, eat another four or five cloves of garlic daily for three months.

ULCERS

For decades, conventional doctors have treated gastric and duodenal ulcers with antacids, dietary changes, and stress reduction. In recent years, researchers have discovered that most ulcers are accompanied by an infection by the germ *Helicobacter pylori,* and treatment with antibiotic agents is now routine for ulcers. One of the drugs used, metronizadole

(Flagyl), is somewhat controversial. Although it will effectively eliminate the helicobacter infection when used in combination with other drugs, it has severe side effects of its own, such as neurological damage and possible cancer. Helicobacter is not even the cause of some ulcers; it is a common resident of the stomach and sometimes does not cause disease there. Thus, heroic attempts to eradicate it may not be necessary, especially with drugs like Flagyl. I had a patient who had been given more than ten courses of Flagyl within a year to treat an ulcer and vaginal infections, and by the end of the year she had nerve damage and multiple sclerosis.

Some medical researchers think that treatment with metronizadole should only be used as a last resort. In one study, ninety patients with duodenal ulcers were treated with medications to reduce the secretion of stomach acid. Twenty-seven of these remained ulcer-free with no further treatment. Forty-seven more had only one or two recurrences of ulcers within a year. Of sixteen that had three or more recurrences, only twelve were infected with helicobacter, and were treated with metronizadole. The researchers concluded that drugs to reduce acid secretion are adequate for most patients.

This raises possibilities for using garlic in the treatment of ulcers. Physicians have prescribed it for gastritis and other intestinal infections since the dawn of recorded history, and experimenters have proven its antibiotic properties. If you have an ulcer and your doctor recommends drug therapy with metronidazole, ask if you can try a more conservative treatment first. One advantage of taking the garlic is that it has side benefits instead of side effects. If the ulcers recur, and laboratory tests confirm that you have helicobacter infection, consider taking the drug treatment.

For ulcer treatment, use one of the potent raw forms in Chapter 14. Don't take capsules, especially enteric-coated ones, because they may bypass the stomach completely and deliver their garlic below the ulcer in the digestive tract.

UNDERWEIGHT

We saw in Chapter 11 that garlic is a tonic. Even if you do not have a specific disease, it can build overall health, improve digestion, increase resistance to disease, and strengthen the system. This property may be helpful in people who are underweight and want to gain weight. The ancient Indians used garlic for this purpose, and even today garlic oils are used in Ayurvedic medicine to help gain weight.

Dr. Vesselin Petkov of Bulgaria tested the hypothesis that garlic could increase weight in experiments on pigs and cows. He fed the pigs a dose of garlic equivalent to three to four cloves of garlic for a 180-pound man. In ten weeks, the garlic-fed pigs had put on 13 percent more weight than pigs on a regular diet. They put on this weight while actually eating less food than the others. Presumably, the garlic improved both digestion and metabolism. Petkov followed up the study on calves, but with twice the dose—six to eight cloves a day for a 180-pound man. After four months, the calves who ate garlic regularly weighed 12 percent more than the other cows and had also consumed less food.

VAGINAL INFECTIONS

Vaginal infection may be caused either by organisms that are normal residents of the vagina, such as candida yeast overgrowth, or by external microorganisms that are introduced through sexual relations. Itching, irritation, and redness can be severe and can spread to the vulva. Vaginal discharge may or may not be present.

It is important to investigate the cause of vaginal infection, because some infections, such as gonorrhea, can have serious consequences. Also, conditions as simple as a forgotten tampon or as serious as vaginal cancer, can produce the same symptoms. The symptoms may also be caused by allergies, in which case antibiotic treatment, whether conventional or herbal, will not be effective.

The most common infectious agents are *trichomonas, candida,* and *gardnerella.* These cause no severe or life-threatening pathology, but they can cause unrelenting discomfort. Trichomonas is sexually transmitted, and male partners may carry the infection without having symptoms themselves, so the partner should be checked and treated if necessary in persistent infections.

Tori Hudson, N.D., Professor of Gynecology at the National College of Naturopathic Medicine in Portland, Oregon, often recommends a garlic clove suppository for vaginal infections. "Peel the outer paper-like skin on the clove," she says, "but don't nick the clove." Cutting or nicking a garlic clove releases the irritating substances in garlic, and could irritate the vagina. Some individuals are especially sensitive to "garlic burns." Hudson says the clove can be used for about half a day, either during the day or night. If a woman doesn't want to retrieve it with her fingers, she can use olive oil-soaked gauze around the clove and thread it like a tampon. Hudson alternates day or night garlic treatment with something soothing, like acidophilus capsules, during the other half of the twenty-four-hour cycle. Inserted in the vagina, the gelatin capsule dissolves and releases beneficial acidophilus bacteria.

For serious yeast overgrowth, Hudson recommends a garlic clove suppository also inserted into the anus. The normal yeast population of the intestine and vagina can become overgrown after antibiotic or cortisone therapy or other causes that disrupt the normal balance of friendly bacteria in the gut and vagina. It is common in such cases that yeast from the anus continues to reinfect the vagina, working its way along the "sweat track" between the two orifices. The garlic suppository in the anus fights the yeast overgrowth there.

Dr. Mary Bove of Brattleboro, Vermont, has further suggestions for chronic yeast infection. She says it's important to treat the yeast infection in the intestines as well as in the vagina. For this purpose, she suggests enteric-coated forms of garlic, widely available commercially at health food stores. These capsules have a coating that ensures that the garlic is released deep in the intestines where the yeast infections lie and not digested in the upper tract. She also recommends external treatment of the perineum, the space between the anus and the vagina, with an herbal wash to prevent the spread of yeast from the anus to the vagina. Her patients use thyme, yarrow, or rosemary tea in a squirt bottle, and wash the area after urinating or defecating, then pat the orifices dry with toilet paper. If people do not want to go to the bother of making the tea, they can put a half teaspoon of tincture of equal parts of garlic, echinacea, myrrh, and calendula in an eight-ounce squirt bottle and fill with water. "It's unbelievable how such a simple treatment can make a dramatic difference for yeast infections," say Bove.

A garlic clove suppository will sometimes come out on its own, unnoticed. Amanda McQuade Crawford, M.N.I.M.H. of California tells the story of a woman who called her one night fearful after being unable to find the garlic clove.

"She was profoundly disturbed that it might have ascended into the mysterious depths of her being," Crawford relates. She suggests that the clove sometimes breaks down partially in the vagina, and is evacuated unnoticed with the morning urination or bowel movement. Crawford also plays down the danger of the clove decomposing in the vagina and causing further infection. "I've never run into this, with hundreds of patients, including young girls, college girls, and sexually active women of all ages," she states. Some conventional doctors warn of this as a potential problem. The case of the woman with the missing clove had a happy ending, as it turns out. Crawford suggested that the clove probably came out unnoticed in the toilet, but instructed her to watch for any sign of irritation or infection. The woman continued the garlic treatments and her yeast infection cleared up without the use of over-the-counter or prescription medicines, which had not worked for her in the past.

Another way to use garlic for vaginal infection comes from Chris Deatherage, N.D., of Missouri. He suggests mixing three garlic cloves in a blender with three or four cups of water, and using it as a douche. "That works wonders," he claims. This approach frees the powerfully antibiotic constituent allicin from garlic. For more details, see Chapter 12. Allicin has been proven in dozens of clinical trials to have antibiotic properties against a wide variety of infectious organisms, including trichomonas and candida yeast.

WORMS

Pinworm infestations are common in the young, affecting about 20 percent of the population of school-age children. They usually cause no symptoms, but they may cause anal itching or even vaginal itching in young girls. Only very active cases with massive infection require energetic treatment with drugs. Herbal master Dr. R. F. Weiss of Germany recommends against using pharmaceutical drugs for less serious cases, saying that herbal treatments are adequate. He suggests instead a garlic enema, made from one clove of garlic chopped up and boiled for ten minutes in a half-pint of water. Garlic is given orally at the same time. He suggests a treatment like this once a week. Dr. Chris Deatherage of Missouri recommends a little stronger treatment: two cloves blended in water and not heated. Administer it with a bulb syringe. Deatherage says that with this treatment, no oral use is necessary, and the worms are cleared up after one or two treatments. In one clinical trial in India, a three-week course of simple garlic tablets was very helpful for worms.

CHAPTER 16

Conclusion: Garlic and the Cost of Medical Care

Since the time of the Romans, garlic has carried the name *poor man's heal-all,* first in Latin, then in Arabic and Persian, and finally in English. The name, which still appears in English and Arabic herbals, has stuck for almost two thousand years, in cultures from England, throughout Europe, across Africa, the Middle East, the Indian subcontinent, Southeast Asia, and as far as Malaysia and Indonesia. Garlic earned this name in places and times when official medicines were too expensive for the common people, who turned to garlic instead. Ironically, garlic has proven its worth over time—its higher-priced competitors of the past are all forgotten, while garlic wins respect today even from conventional physicians. For household economics in today's medical marketplace, the need for a simple and inexpensive "cure-all" for the major diseases of our day is just as important as it was in the past.

HOUSEHOLD ECONOMICS

Garlic is so inexpensive, especially if you take it in one of the homemade forms in Chapter 14, that you can treat a family of six for less than fifty cents a day. That would be even less if you planted your own garlic patch in your backyard. The family cost savings are not simply limited to the low cost of garlic. Garlic can prevent many diseases, from the common cold to cancer, and all of these have out-of-pocket costs from a few dollars to hundreds of thousands of dollars in terms of lost family income, even if you have good health insurance coverage. Using garlic, with your physician's permission, as a substitute for drug prescriptions in conditions such as high blood pressure, acne, vaginal infections, or bronchitis could also dramatically lower personal health care costs and drug side effects at the same time.

PUBLIC HEALTH

The widespread promotion of garlic consumption as a public health policy could dramatically affect health costs in the United States. A study published in the *Southern Medical Journal* found that dietary treatments to lower serum cholesterol are dramatically more cost-effective than drug treatments.

In the table on the next page, the negative numbers indicate that dietary therapy saves money because expensive conditions like heart attacks, strokes, and cancer are reduced. The cost of the foods or supplements are more than repaid by reduced medical expenses later. The researchers did not investigate garlic in this study, but its cost would logically be at or below the cost of dietary advice. We see in Chapter 9

RELATIVE EXPENSE OF SAVING A YEAR OF LIFE IN PATIENTS WITH ELEVATED SERUM CHOLESTEROL	
Dietary advice	–$2536
Niacin	–$1234
Psyllium husk	–$642
Lovastatin	$50,510
Colestipol	$73,406
Colestyramine	$92,603
Gemfribrozol	$108,826

that garlic in any of its forms can lower cholesterol. Imagine the savings, on a national level, if physicians would prescribe garlic and dietary changes as a first resort to lower cholesterol and only prescribe the more expensive drugs if the first method did not work.

Even a modest reduction of cardiovascular disease with garlic could save billions of dollars annually in the United States. The cost of a heart attack is in the range of $25,000 to $75,000 per attack. We saw in Chapters 9 and 15 that garlic can prevent heart attacks and especially second heart attacks—one trial showed only half the deaths from a second heart attack in a group that took garlic each day for three years. Only seven thousand heart attacks prevented a year—that's less than one-tenth of one percent of the total heart attacks in the United States—would save enough money to provide every person in the United States with a half-clove of garlic a day, enough to reduce heart attacks.

AIDS TREATMENT

The AIDS epidemic continues to grow in the United States and worldwide, and its treatment is rapidly becoming unaffordable, both to people with AIDS and to the health care system as a whole. We saw in Chapters 2 and 5 that clinics using Chinese and naturopathic medicine in the United States use garlic as their main agent for prevention and treatment of the opportunistic infections that accompany AIDS. The Immune Enhancement Project in Portland, Oregon, uses garlic this way and can offer a full range of natural health services, including office visits, acupuncture, therapeutic massage, Chinese herbal treatments, and vitamin supplements for one hundred dollars a month to clients. Compare this to the cost of some AIDS drugs, which are more than one thousand dollars a month, just for the medication, and which are no more effective than the natural treatments.

POOR MAN'S PLAGUE CURE

In past history, garlic was not just used by the poor to save money; it was used for epidemic diseases for which regular medicine had no cure. The same is true today of the common cold. Colds and flu sweep neighborhoods, workplaces, and schools regularly. Last year in Portland, Oregon, where I live, at one point 40 percent of the students in the public school system were out of school with the flu. Most years, outbreaks are mild, but from time to time extremely virulent strains come along, and some people become seriously ill. Once or twice a century, a major flu epidemic strikes with deadly severity. Two separate epidemics killed tens of millions of people worldwide in the last hundred years. Garlic is an effective preventive or treatment for the flu, whereas conventional medicine has no treatment. Consider keeping it around for regular colds and flu.

Public health officials are also concerned about the possibility of new plague diseases like those of the past coming to haunt us. They are especially concerned about as-yet-undiscovered viruses—consider the unexpected outbreak of the Ebola virus in Zaire, and the subject of the movie *Outbreak*, as well as plagues of drug-resistant bacteria. No one can say for certain if garlic will help fight against future plagues, but we know that, unlike conventional medications, garlic is effective against many viruses and drug-resistant bacteria. I plan to keep some bulbs around my house just in case.

GARLIC IN THE FUTURE

The peasants of Galen's day took garlic instead of the expensive remedies available in the cities then. In retrospect, it seems the peasants got the best of the deal. Today, we've forgotten the other remedies completely, but garlic is still popular throughout the world for the same things it was used for in Galen's day. I suspect that in another two thousand years, today's antibiotics, cholesterol-lowering drugs, and other medicines will be as forgotten as the polypharmacy of the Romans. And I bet we'll still be using garlic.

REFERENCES

Chapter 1

Cook, W. 1869. *The Physio-Medical Dispensatory.*

Eichholz, D. E., W. H. S. Jones, and H. Tackham, trans. 1952-1971. *Pliny Natural History.* Loeb Classical Library.

Felter, H. W., and J. U. Lloyd. *1898. King's American Dispensatory.* Portland, OR: Eclectic Medical Publications.

Fulder, S. 1991. *Garlic: Nature's Original Remedy.* Rochester, VT: Healing Arts Press.

Gunther, R. T. 1959. *Greek Herbal of Dioscorides.* New York: Hafner Publishing Co.

Heinerman, J. 1994. *The Healing Benefits of Garlic: From Pharaobs to Pharmacists.* New Canaan, CT: Keats Publishing.

Madaus, G. 1976. *Lerhbuch der Bioligischen Heilmittel.* Hildesheim, Germany: Georg Olms Verlag.

Manniche, Lisa. 1989. *An Ancient Egyptian Herbal.* Austin: Univ. of Texas Press.

Osol, A., and G. E. Farrar. 1947. *United States Dispensatory.* Philadelphia: J. B. Lippencott Co.

Strehlow, W., and G. Hertzka. 1988. *Hildegard of Bingen's Medicine.* Santa Fe, NM: Bear & Co.

von Deines, H., and H. Grapow. 1954-1973. *Grundriss der Medizin der Alten Agypter.* West Berlin: Westendorf.

Chapter 2

Bensky, D., and A. Gamble. 1986. *Chinese Herbal Medicine Materia Medica.* Seattle: Eastland Press.

Edwards, R., and Zeng Ding-yi, trans. 1989. *Vegetables As Medicine.* Kurunda, Australia: Rams Skull Press.

Hunan Medical College of China. 1980. *Chin Med J* 93:123.

Leung, A. Y. 1984. *Chinese Herbal Remedies.* New York: Phaidon Universe.

Chapter 3

Das, P. K., G. D. Gupta, and A. K. Mishra. 1986. *Current Research on Medicinal Plants of India.* Edited by B. N. Dhawan. New Delhi: Indian National Science Academy.

Frawley, D. 1989. *Ayurvedic Healing.* Salt Lake City: Passage Press.

Frawley, D., and V. Lad. 1986. *Yoga of Herbs.* Santa Fe, NM: Lotus Press..

Nagendra Prasad, P., and Z. Abraham. 1984. *J Econ Tax Bot. 4:*453-474.

Saxena, A. P., and K. M. Vyas. 1983. *J Econ Tax Bot. 4:167-172.*

Singh U., A. M. Wadhani, and B M. Johri. 1983. *Dictionary of Economic Plants of India.* New Delhi: Indian Coun. Agr. Res.

Chapter 4

al-Sayuti. 1993. *Medicine of the Prophet S.A.S. (Tibb-ul-Nabbi) of Al-Suyuti.* Oxford, NY: Chishti Publishing Group.

Chisthi, Hakim G. M. 1988. *The Traditional Healer.* Rochester, VT: Healing Arts Press.

Chisthi, Hakim G. M. 1986. *The Book of Sufi Healing.* Rochester, VT: Healing Arts Press.

Gruner, O. C. 1991. *A Treatise on the Canon of Medicine of Avicenna.* Reprint. Sidney, NY: American Institute of Unani Medicine.

Hitti, P. K., trans. 1987. *An Arab-Syrian Gentleman and Warrior in Period of the Crusades.* Princeton, NJ: Princeton Univ. Press.

Kamal, H. 1975. *Encyclopedia of Islamic Medicine.* Cairo, Egypt: General Egyptian Book Organization.

Chapter 5.

Abdullah T., et al. Jun. 4-9, 1989. Int Conf AIDS. 5:466 (abstract no. Th. B. P. 304).

Abehsera, M. 1995. *Our Earth, Our Cure.* New York: Carol Publishing.

Felter, H. 1985. *The Eclectic Materia Medica, Pharmacology, and Therapeutics.* Reprint. Portland, OR: Eclectic Medical Publications.

Kirchfeld, F., and W. Boyle. 1995. *Nature Doctors.* Portland, OR: Medicina Biologica.

Standish L., et al. 1992. *J Naturopath Med.* 3(1): 42-64.

Thrash, A., and C. Thrash. 1981. *Home Remedies: Hydrotherapy, Massage, Charcoal, and Other Simple Treatments.* Seale, AL: Thrash Publications.

Chapter 6

British Herbal Medicine Association. 1983. *British Herbal Pharmacopoeia.* London: BHMA.

Hintzelmann, Nauyn-Schmiedebergs. 1935. *Arch F Exp Path U Pharm.* 178:480.

Kraemer. 1936. *Psch Neurol Wschr.* 3:28.

Madaus, G. 1976. *Lerhbuch der bioligischen Heilmittel.* Reprint. Hildesheim, Germany: Georg Olms Verlag.

Payer, L. 1988. *Medicine and Culture.* New York: Henry Holt and Co.

Strecker. 1930. *Zbl Gynak* 54:1690.

Weiss, R. F. 1988. *Herbal Medicine* (trans. from the Sixth German Edition of *Lehrbuch der Phytotherapie).* Beaconsfield, England: Beaconsfield Publishers.

Chapter 7

Crellin, J. K., and J. Philpott. 1990. *Herbal Medicine Past and Present. 2 Vols.* Durham, NC: Duke University Press.

Messegue, M. 1991. *Of People and Plants.* Rochester, VT: Healing Arts Press.

Moore, M. 1990. *Los Remedios.* Santa Fe, NM: Red Crane Books.

Petkov, V. 1986. *J Ethnopharmacol* 15:121-132.

Chapter 8

Antibiotic Properties

Adetumbi M., G. T. Javor, and B. H. Lau. Sep, 1986. *Antimicrob Agents Chemother.* 499–501.

Adetumbi, M. A., and B. H. Lau. Nov, 1983. *Med Hypotheses* 12(3): 227–37.

Anesini, C., and C. Perez. Jun, 1993. *J Ethnopharmacol* 39(2): 119–28.

Appleton, J. A., and M. R. Tansey. Jul-Aug, 1975. *Mycologia* 67(4): 882–5.

Barone, F. E., and M. R. Tansey. Jul-Aug, 1977. *Mycologia* 69(4): 793–825.

Bilgrami, K. S., K. K. Sinha, and A. K. Sinha. Jun, 1992. *Indian J Med Res.* 96:171–5.

Borukh, I. F., et al. May-Jun, 1975. *Prikl Biokhim Mikrobiol* 11(3): 478–9.

Borukh, I. F., et al. Sep-Oct, 1974. *Vopr Pitan* 20(5): 80–1.

Chen, H. C., M. D. Chang, and T. J. Chang. Aug, 1985. *Chung Hua Min Kuo Wei Sheng Wu Chi Mien I Hsueh Tsa Chih* 18(3): 190–5.

Caporaso, N., S. M. Smith, and R. H. Eng. May, 1983. *Antimicrob Agents Chemother* 23(5): 700–2.

Chowdhury, A. K., et al. Jan, 1991. *Indian J Med Res.* 93:33–6.

Conner, D. E., and L. R. Beuchat. Feb, 1984. *Appl Environ Microbiol* 47(2): 229–33.

Dankert, J., et al. Oct, 1979. *Zentralbl Bakteriol* 245(1–2): 229–39.

Davis, L. E., J. Shen, and R. E. Royer. Dec, 1994. *Planta Med.* 60(6): 546–9.

Davis, L. E., J. K. Shen, and Y. Cai. Apr, 1990. *Antimicrob Agents Chemother.* 34(4): 651–3.

Didry, N., L. Dubreuil, and M. Pinkas. 1992. *Pharm Acta Helv.* 67(5–6): 148–51.

Didry, N., M. Pinkas, and L. Dubreuil. Oct, 1987. *Pharmazie* 42(10): 687–8.

Feldberg, R. S., et al. Dec, 1988. *Antimicrob Agents Chemother* 32(12): 1763–8.

Fletcher, R. D., B. Parker, and M. Hassett. 1974. *Folia Microbiol* (Praha) 19(6): 494–7.

Antiviral Properties

Esanu, V. Oct-Dec, 1984. *Virologie* 35(4): 281–93.

Esanu, V. Jan-Mar, 1981. *Virologie* 32(1): 57–77.

Guo, N. L., et al. Feb, 1993. *Chin Med J (Engl)* 106(2): 93–6.

Nagai, K. Apr, 1973. *Kansenshogaku Zasshi* 47(4): 111–5.

Tatarintsev, A., et al. Jul 19-24, 1992. Int Conf AIDS. 8(3): 39 (abstract no. PuA 6173).

Tatarintsev, A. V., et al. 1992. *Vestn Ross Akad Med Nauk* (11–12): 6–10.

Tsai, Y., et al. Oct, 1985. *Planta Med.* (5):460–1.

Weber, N. D., et al. Oct, 1992. *Planta Med.* 58(5): 417–23.

Immune-Stimulating Properties

Abdullah, T. H., et al. Jun 4-9, 1989. Int Conf AIDS. 5:466 (abstract no. Th B. P. 304).

Abdullah, T. H., D. V. Kirkpatrick, and J. Carter. 1989. *Dtsch Zschr Onkol* 21:52–53.

Feng, Z. H., et al. 1994. *J Tongji Med Univ.* 14(3): 142–7.

Kandil, O., et al. 1988. *Arch AIDS Res.* 1230–231.

Morioka, N., et al. "A protein fraction from aged garlic extract enhances cytotoxicity and proliferation of human lymphocytes mediated by interleukin-2 and concanavalin A."

Reeve, V. E., et al. Dec, 1993. *Photochem Photobiol.* 58(6): 813–7.

Takeyama, H., et al. 1993. *Oncology* 50(1): 63–9.

Chapter 9

Antioxidation

Fu, N. Aug, 1993. *Chung Kuo I Hsueh Ko Hsueh Yuan Hsueh* Pao 15(4): 295–301.

Heinle, H., and E. Betz. May, 1994. *Arzneimittelforschung* 44(5): 614–7.

Horie, T., et al. Oct, 1992. *Planta Med.* 58(5): 468–9.

Imai, J., et al. "Antioxidant and radical scavenging effects of aged garlic extract and its constituents."

Kourounakis, P. N., and E. A. Rekka. Nov, 1991. *Res Commun Chem Pathol Pharmacol.* 74(2): 249–52.

Lewin, G., and I. Popov. May, 1994. *Arzneimittelforschung* 44(5): 604–7.

Perchellet, J. P., et al. Oct, 1986. *Cancer Biochem Biophys* 8(4): 299–312.

Phelps, S., and W. S. Harris. May, 1993. *Lipids* 28(5): 475–7.

Popov, I., A. Blumstein, and G. Lewin. May, 1994. *Arzneimittelforschung* 44(5): 602–4.

Rekka, E. A., and P. N. Kourounakis. Jul, 1994. *Pharmazie* 49(7): 539–40.

Stavric, B. Oct, 1994. *Clin Biochem.* 27(5): 319–32.

Atherosclerosis

Kiesewetter, H., et al. May, 1993. *Clin Investig.* 71(5): 383–6.

Mirhadi, S. A., S. Singh, and P. P. Gupta. Feb, 1991. *Indian J Exp Biol.* 29(2): 162–8.

Sainani, G. S., et al. May, 1979. *Jpn Heart J.* 20(3): 351–7.

Blood Pressure

Gadkari, J. V., and V. D. Joshi. Jul, 1991. *J Postgrad Med.* 37(3): 128–31.

McMahon, F. G., and R. Vargas. Jul-Aug, 1993. *Pharmacotherapy* 13(4): 406–7.

Osol, A., and G. E. Farrar. 1947. *U.S. Dispensatory.* Philadelphia: J. B. Lippencott Company.

Silagy, C. A., and H. A. Neil. Apr, 1994. *J Hypertens.* 12(4): 463–8.

Blood Thinning

Block, E., et al. 1984. *J Am Chem Soc.* 106:8295.

Bordia, A. 1978. *Atherosclerosis* 30(4): 355–360.

Chutani, S. K., and A. Bordia. 1981. *Atherosclerosis* 38(3-4): 417–421.

Elwood, P. C., et al. Aug, 1993. *Blood Caogul Fibrinolysis* 4(4): 529–36.

Kiesewetter, H., et al. Apr, 1991. *Int J Clin Pharmacol Ther Toxicol.* 29(4): 151–5.

Makheja, A. N., et al. 1980. *Adv Prostaglandin Thromboxane* Res. 6:309–12.

Makheja, A. N., J. Y. Vanderhoek, and J. M. Bailey. 1979. *Lancet.* 1:781.

Mohammad, S. F., and S. C. Woodward. Dec 15, 1986. *Thromb Res.* 44(6): 793–806.

Sinaini, G. S., D. B. Desai, and K. N. More. 1976. *Lancet.* 9:575–576.

Srivastava, K. C., 1984. *Prostaglandin Leukotriene Med.* 13:227–235.

Cholesterol

Abuirmeileh, N., et al. 1991. *FASEB Journal* 5(6): A1756.

Davey Smith, G., F. Song, and T. A. Sheldon. 1993. *BMJ.* 306:1367–73.

Gadhari, J. V., and V. D. Joshi. Jul, 1991. *J Postgrad Med.* 37(3): 128–31.

Gebhardt., R. Jul, 1993. *Lipids* 28(7): 613–9.

Holzgartner, H., U. Schmidt, and U. Kuhn. Dec, 1992. *Arzneimittelforschung* 42(12): 1473–7.

Jacob, B. G., and P. Schwandt. Mar, 1992. *Dtsch Med Wochenschr* 6;117(10): 397–8.

Kenzelmann, R., and F. Kade. Sep, 1993. *Arzneimittelforschung* 43(9): 978–81.

Rotzsch, W., et al. Oct, 1992. *Arzneimittelforschung* 42(10): 1223–7.

Sendl, A., et al. May, 1992. Atherosclerosis 94(1): 79–85.

Silagy, C., and A. Neil. Jan-Feb, 1994. *J R Coll Physicians Lond* 28(1): 39–45.

Warshafsky, S., R. S. Kamer, and S. L. Sivak. Oct., 1993. *Ann Intern Med.* 119(7 Pt 1): 599–605.

Yeh, Y. Y., and S. M. Yeh. Mar, 1994. *Lipids* 29(3): 189–93.

Chapter 10

Baer, A. R., and M. J. Wargovich. Sep 15, 1989. *Cancer Res.* 49(18): 5073–6.

Belman, S. 1983. *Carcinogenesis* 4(8): 1063–1065.

Belman, S., et al. 1987. *Proc AACR* 28:166.

Bogin, E., and M. Abrams. 1976. *Food Cosmet Toxicol.* 14(5): 417–419.

Cheng H., and T. Tung. 1981. *J Formosan Med Assoc.* 80:385–393.

Choy, Y. M., et al. 1983. *Am J Chin Med.* 11(1–4): 69–73.

Cipriana, F., E. Buiatti, and D. Palli. Sep-Oct, 1991. *Ital J Gastroenterol* 23(7): 429–435.

Criss, W.E., et al. 1982. *Proceedings, 66th Annu. Meet. FASEB.* Abstract 74:281.

Dausch, J. G., and D. W. Nixon. 1990. *Prev Med.* 19;346–361.

Devasagayam, T. P., C. K. Pushpendran, and J. Eapen. 1982. *Ind J Exp Biol.* 20(5): 430–432

Doll, R., and R., Rao. 1981. *J Natl. Cancer Inst.* 66:1191–1308.

Feng, Z. H., et al. 1994. *J Tongji Med Univ.* 14(3): 142–7.

Fujiwara, M., and T. Natata. 1967. *Nature* 216:83–84.

Haenszel, W., M. Kurihara, and M. Segi. 1972. *J Natl Cancer Inst.* 49: 969–988.

Hikino, H., et al., 1986. *Planta Med.* 163–168.

Hu, P. J., and M. J. Wargovich. Sep 15, 1989. *Cancer Lett* 47(1–2): 153–8.

Ip, C., D. J. Lisk, and J. A. Scimeca. 1994. *Cancer Res(Suppl).* 54:1957s–1959s.

Ip, C., D. J. Lisk, and G. S. Stoewsand. 1992. *Nutr Canc.* 17(3): 280–286.

Ip, C., and H. E. Ganther. 1992. *Cancer Chemoprevention.* Ed. L. Wattenberg, M. Lipkin, C. W. Boone, and G. J. Kelloff. 195–203. Boca Raton. FL: CRC Press.

Ip, C. 1981. *Cancer Res.* 41:2683–2686.

Kimura, Y., and K. Yamamoto. 1964. *GANN* 55:325–329.

Knasmuller, S., et al. 1989. *Environ Mol Mutagen* 13:357–365.

Kroning, F. 1964. *Acta Unio Contra Cancrum* 20(3): 855–856.

Lau, B. 1988. *Garlic for Your Health.* Wilmot, WI: Lotus Light Publications.

Marchall, M. V., et al. 1979. *Cancer Lett.* 7:331.

Nakagawa, S., et al. 1985. *In Vitro* 34(3): 303–309.

Nakata, T. 1973. *Jpn J Hyg.* 27(6): 538–543.

Nishino, H., et al. 1990. *Cancer Journal* 3(1): 20–21.

Scharfenberg, K., R. Wagner, K. G. Wagner. 1990. *Cancer Lett.* 53:103–108.

Steinmetz, K. A., et al. 1994. *Am J Epidemiol.* 139(1): 1–13.

Sumiyoshi, H. and M. J. Wargovich. Aug 15, 1990. *Cancer Res.* 50(16): 5084–7.

Tadi, P. P., R. W. Teel, and B. H. S. Lau. 1991. *Nutr Canc.* 15:87–95.

Tanaka, M. 1982. *Japanese J New Remedies* 31:1349.

Von Euler, H., and G. Lindeman. 1949. *Ark F Kemi.* 87–90.

Wang, Z., et al. 1990. *J Natl Cancer Inst.* 82(6): 478–485.

Wargovich, M. J., and V. W. S. Eng. 1989. *Nutr Cancer* 12(2): 189–194.

Wargovich, M. J., et al. Dec 1, 1988. *Cancer Res.* 48(23): 6872–5.

Wargovich, M. J. Mar, 1987. *Carcinogenesis* 8(3): 487–9.

Wargovich, M. J., and M. T. Goldberg. 1985. *Mutat Res.* 143:127–129.

Weisberger, A. S., and J. Pensky. 1957. *Science* 126:1112–1114.

Yamasaki, T., R. W. Teel, and B. H. S. Lau. Aug, 1991. *Cancer Lett.* 59(2): 89–94.

Yang, C. S., Z. Y. Wang, and J. Y. Hong. 1994. *Adv Exp Med Biol.* 354;113–22.

You, W. C., et al. 1991. *IARC Sci Publ.* 105:338.

Zheng, W., et al. Jul 15, 1992. *Am J Epidemiol.* 136(2): 178–191.

Chapter 11

Hasegawa, Y., et al. 1983. *Japanese J New Remedies* 32:365.

Imai, J., et al. 1994. *Planta Med.* 60:417–420.

Kajiyama, G., Hiroshima University Group. 1982. *Japanese J Clin Rep.* 16:1515.

Kawashima, H., Y. Ochiai, and H. Shuzenji. "Anti-fatigue effect of aged garlic extract in athletic club students."

Lau, B. 1988. *Garlic for Your Health.* Wilmot, WI: Lotus Light Publications.

Miyoshi, A., et al. 1984. *Shinryou to Sin-yaku.* 21:1806–1820.

Moriguchi, T., et al. 1994. *Biol Pharm Bull* 17(2): 1589–1594.

Okada, K., and H. Miyagaki. 1983. *Clinical Report* 17:2173–2183.

Saxena, K. K., et al. 1980. *Indian J Physiol Pharmacol.* 24:233.

Takasugi, N., et al. 1984. *Oyo Yakuri-Pharmacometrics* 28:991, 1984.

Takasugi, N., K. Mira, and T. Fuwa. 1986. *Oyo Yakuri-Pharmacometrics* 31:967.

Tanaka, M. 1982. *Japanese J New Remedies* 31:1349.

Toriyama, M. 1983. *Jap J Jiobirinsho* 76(2): 231.

Yokoyama, K., et al. 1986. *Oyo Yakuri-Pharmacometrics* 31:977.

Chapter 12

Augusti, K. T., and M. E. Benaim. 1974. *Clin Chem Acta.* 60:121.

Barone, F. E., and M. R. Tansey. Jul-Aug, 1977. *Mycologia* 69(4): 793-825.

Block, E., et al. 1984. *J Am Chem Soc.* 106:8295.

Borukh, I. F., et al. Sep-Oct, 1984. *Vopr Pitan.* 0(5): 80—1.

Brahmachari, M. D., and K. T. Augusti. 1962. *J Pharm Pharmacol.* 14:254, 617.

Chowdhury, A. K., et al. Jan, 1991. *Indian J Med Res.* 93:33-6.

Devasagayam, T. P., C. K. Puspendran, and J. Eapen. 1982. *Ind J Exp Biol.* 20(5): 430-432.

Feldberg, R. S., et al. Dec, 1988. *Antimicrob Agents Chemother.* 32(12): 1763—8.

Feng, Z. H., et al. 1994. *J Tongi Med Univ.* 14(3): 142-7.

Focke, M., A. Feld, and K. Lichtenthaler. Feb 12, 1990. *FEBS Lett.* 261(1): 106—8.

Imai, J., et al. Oct, 1994. *Planta Med.* 60(5): 417-20.

Ip, C., D. J. Lisk, and G. S. Stoewsand. 1992. *Nutr Canc.* 17(3): 280-286.

Jain, R. C., and C. R. Vyas. 1974. *Brit Med* J. 2 730.

Morioka, N., et al., "A protein fraction from aged garlic extract enhances cytotoxicity and proliferation of human lymphocytes mediated by interleukin 2 and concanavalin A."

Nakagava, S., et al. 1985. *In Vitro* 34(3): 303-309.

Nishino, H., et al. 1990. *Cancer Journal* 3(1): 20-21.

Rekka, E.A., and P.N. Kourounakis. Jul, 1994. *Pharmazie* 49(7): 539-40.

San-Blas, G., 1993. *J Med Vet Mycol.* 31(2): 133—41.

Scharfenberg, K., R. Wanger, and K. G. Wagner. 1990. *Cancer Lett.* 53:103–108.

Chapter 13

Brenner, S., and R. Wolf. 1994. *Dermatology* 189(4): 337—9.

Burden, A. D., et al. 1994. *Contact Dermatitis* 30(5): 299—300.

Burnham, B. E. Jan, 1995. *Plast Reconstr Surg.* 95(1): 213.

Chutani, S. K., and A. Bordia. 1981. *Atherosclerosis* 38(3-4): 417—421.

Garty, B. Z. 1993. *Pediatrics* 91(3): 659—9.

Gupta, M. K., et al. 1993. *Int J Cardiol.* 38(3): 333.

Hasegava, Y., et al. 1983. *Japanese J New Remedies* 32:365.

Lampe, K. F., and M. A. McCann. 1985. *AMA Handbook of Poisonous and Injurious Plants.* Chicago: American Medical Association.

Lawson, L. L., Z. J. Wang, and B. G. Hughes. 1991. *Planta Med.* 57:363–371.

Lee, T. Y., and T. H. Lam. 1991. *Contact Dermatitis* 24(3): 193—6.

Lembo, G., et al. 1991. *Contact Dermatitis* 25(5):330—1.

McFadden, J. P., I. R. White, and R. J. Rycroft. 1992. *Contact Dermatitis* 27(5): 333—4.

Nakagawa, S., et al. 1980. *J Toxicol Sci.* 5(91).

Shashikanth, S., C. Basappa, and V. S. Murthy. 1986. *Nutr Reports International* 33:313.

Svensson, A., et al. 1991. *Lakartidningen* 88(9): 733—4.

Chapter 14

Fulder, S., and J. Blackwood. 1991. *Garlic: Nature's Original Remedy.* Rochester, VT: Healing Arts Press.

Heinerman, J. 1994. *The Healing Benefits of Garlic.* New Canaan, CT: Keats Publishing.

Lawson, L. L., Z. J. Wang, and B..G. Hughes. 1991. *Planta Med.* 57:363–371.

Chapter 15

AIDS

Abdullah, T., et al. Jun 4-9, 1989. Int Conf AIDS. 5:466 (abstract no. Th. B.P.304).

Abdullah, T. H., D. V. Kirkpatrick, and J. Carter. 1989. *Dtsch Zschr Onkol.* 21:52—53.

Delaha, E. C., and V. L. Garagusi. 1985. *Antimicrob Agents Chemother* 27(4): 485—486.

Deshpande, R. G., et al. Oct, 1993. *J Antimicrob Chemother* 32(4): 623—6.

Fronting, R. A., and G. S. Bulmer. 1978. *Mycopathologia* 70:397—405.

Gowen, S. L., et al. Jun 6-11, 1993. Int Conf AIDS. 9(1):497 (abstract no. PO-B29-2174).

Hunan Medical College of China. 1980. *Chin Med J.* 93:123.

Rao, R. R., et al. 1946. *Nature* 157.

Standish, L., et al. 1992. *J Naturopath Med.* 3(1): 42—64.

Tatarintsev, A. V., P. V. Vrzhets, and D. E. Ershov. 1992. *Vestn Ross Akad Med Nauk.* (11—12):6—10.

Tatarintsev, A., et al. Jul 19-24, 1992. Int Conf AIDS. 8(3):39 (abstract no. PuA 6173).

Tsai, Y., et al. 1985. *Planta Medica* 5:460—461.

Appetite Loss, Constipation, Fatigue

Hasegawa, Y., et al. 1983. *Japanese J New Remedies* 32:365.

Atherosclerosis, Blood Clots

See the references at the end of Chapter 9.

Asthma

British Herbal Medicine Association. 1983. *British Herbal Pharmacopoeia.* London, England: BHMA.

Strehlow, W., and G. Hertzka. 1988. *Hildegard of Bingen's Medicine.* Santa Fe, NM: Bear and Company.

Bronchitis

Ziment, I. 1985. *Advances in Chinese Medicinal Materials Research.* Ed. H. M. Chang, et al. 193-202. Singapore: World Scientific Publishing.

Cancer

See the references at the end of Chapter 10.

Candida, Vaginal Infections

Adetumbi, M., G. T. Javor, and B. H. Lau. Sep, 1986. *Antimicrob Agents Chemother* 30(3): 499—501.

Barone, F. E., and M. R. Tansey. Jul-Aug, 1977. *Mycologia* 69(4): 793—825.

Caporaso, N., S. M. Smith, and R. H. Eng. May, 1983. *Antimicrob Agents Chemother* 23(5): 700—2.

Conner, D. E., and L. R. Beuchat. Feb, 1984. *Appl Environ Microbiol.* 47(2): 229—33.

Ghannoum, M. A. Feb, 1990. *J Appl Bacteriol.* 68(2): 163—9.

Ghannoum, M. A. Nov, 1988. *J Gen Microbiol.* 134(Pt 11): 2917—24.

Prasad, G., and V. D. Sharma. 1980. *Brit Vet J.* 136:448—451.

Sandhu, D. K., M. K. Warraich, and S. Singh. Dec, 1980. *Mykosen* 23(12): 691—8.

Tynecka, Z., and Z. Gos. 1973. *Acta Microbiol Pol* [B]. 5(1): 51—62.

Yamada, Y., and K. Azuma. Apr, 1977. *Antimicrob Agents Chemother* 11(4): 743—9.

Kabilik, J. 1970. *Pharmazie* 25, 266.

Chemotherapy/Radiotherapy

Tanaka, M. 1982. *Japanese J New Remedies* 31:1349.

Toriyama, M. 1983. *Jap J Jiobirinsho* 76(2): 231.

Claudication

Kiesewetter, H., et al. May, 1993. *Clin Investig.* 71(5): 383—6.

Diabetes

Augusti., K. T., and M. E. Benaim. 1974. *Clin Chem Acta.* 60:121.

Bever, B. O., and G. R. Zahnd. *Quart J Crude Drug Res.*

Brahmachari, M. D., and K. T. Augusti. 1962. *J Pharm Pharmacol.* 14:254,617.

Jain, R. C., and C. R. Vyas. Jul, 1975. *Am J Clin Nutr.* 28(7): 684—5.

Madaus, G. 1976. *Lerhbuch der bioligischen Heilmittel.* Hildesheim, Germany: Georg Olms Verlag.

Sheela, C. G., and K. T. Augusti. 1992. *Indian J Exp Biol.* 30(6): 523—526.

Dysentery

Chowdhury, A. K., et al. Jan, 1991. *Indian J Med Res.* 93:33—6.

Ear Problems

Diamant, M., and R. Diamant. 1974. *Arch Otol.* 100:226—232.

Mygind, N., et al. 1981. *Clin Otol.* 6:5—13.

Van Buchem, F. L., J. H. M. Dunk, and M. A. Van't Hof. Oct 24, 1981. *Lancet.* 883—887.

Hangovers

Takasugi, N., et al. 1984. *Oyo Yakuri-Pharmacometrics* 28:991.

Heart Attacks

Chutani, S. K., and A. Bordia. 1981. *Atherosclerosis* 38(3–4): 417–421.

Isensee, H., B. Rietz, and R. Jacob. Feb, 1993. *Arzneimittelforschung* 43(2): 94–8.

Rietz, B., et al. Feb 17, 1993. *Mol Cell Biochem.* 119(12): 143–50.

Heavy-metal Poisoning

Hanafy, M. S., et al. 1994. *Deutsch Tierarztl Wochenschr* 101(4): 157–158.

Kitahara, S. Kokai PATENT NO. 77 72810 06/17/77 (Fujinaga Pharmaceutical Co., Ltd.) Japan.

Lau, B. 1988. *Garlic for Your Health.* Wilmot, WI: Lotus Light Publications.

Petkov, V. 1986. *J Ethnopharmacol.* 15:121–132.

High Blood Pressure

McMahon, F. G., and R. Vargas. Jul-Aug, 1993. *Pharmacotherapy* 13(4): 406–7.

Silagy, C. A., and H. A. Neil. Apr, 1994. *J Hypertens.* 12(4): 463–8.

High Cholesterol

Lau, B. 1988. *Garlic for Your Health.* Wilmot, WI: Lotus Light Publications.

Silagy, C., and A. Neil. Jan-Feb, 1994. *J R Coll Physicians Lond* 28(1): 39–45.

Influenza

Nagai, K. 1973. *Japan J Infect Dis.* 47:321.

Tsai, Y., et al. 1985. *Planta Medica.* (5):460–461.

Nicotine Withdrawal

Meyer, *E. 1935. Pflanzliche Therapie.* Leipsig.

Tuberculosis, Corns, Nosebleed

Edwards, R., and Z. Ding-yi, trans. 1989. *Vegetables As Medicine.* Kurunda, Australia: Rams Skull Press.

Liu, D. H. 1986. *Zhongjiyikan* 21(2): 121–123.

Ulcers

Hu, P. J., and M. J. Wargovich. 1990. *Chin J Oncol.* 12(6): 429–431.

Kim, N. Y., et al. July, 1994. *Korean J Intern Med.* 9(2): 72–9.

Neeman, A., and U. Kadish. Jul, 1994. *J Clin Gastroenterol.* 19(1): 179.

Nagai, K., et al. 1972. *Japan J Clinical Report* 6:1536.

Underweight

Petkov, V. 1986. *J Ethnopharmacol* 15:121–132.

Petkov, V., E. Kadiiski, and N. Nikolov. 1965. *Zivotnovadni Nauki* 2(1): 105–109 [Bulgarian language].

Worms

Gupta, R., and N. K. Sharma. 1991. *Ind J Nematol* 21(1): 14–18.

Petkov, V., and G. Genov. *Bull NIEM* 2:153–160 (Bulgarian language).

Weiss, R. F. 1988. *Herbal Medicine* (Translated from the Sixth German Edition of Lehrbuch der Phytotherapie). Beaconsfield, England: Beaconsfield Publishers.

INDEX

THE AUTHOR

Paul Bergner, the author, strongly believes that Mother Nature is the world's greatest healer. His conviction is based on intense research and supported by scientific evidence and proof. He is the editor of *Medical Herbalism* and *Clinical Nutrition Update*, and a faculty member at the Rocky Mountain Center for Botanical Studies in Boulder, Colorado, USA. He was the founding editor of *The Naturopath Physician* magazine and has been a contributing editor for *Natural Health, The Nutrition* and *Dietary Consultant*, and *Health World*. He is co-author of several books on herbal medicine, including *Safety, Effectiveness*, and *Cost Effectiveness in Nuturopathic Medicine* and author of *Twelve Powerful Herbs*.